Who Has the Last Word?

CUTTING THROUGH SATAN'S LIES
WITH THE TRUTH OF GOD'S WORD

Michelle J. Goff

Iron Rose Sister Ministries

Michelle J. Goff / CreateSpace
Iron Rose Sister Ministries
www.IronRoseSister.com
1-501-593-4849

Book Layout ©2013 BookDesignTemplates.com

Who Has the Last Word? / Michelle J. Goff.—1st ed.
ISBN 978-0-9963602-4-1 (sc)
ISBN 978-0-9963602-5-8 (e)

Contents

To my friends and family who have spoken truth into my life, and, more importantly, pointed me to the Author of Truth.

Acknowledgements

First and foremost, my thanks go to God, the Alpha and Omega, who has the first and last word, always.

And thanks to you for your patience in the publication of this book. Thus far, this one has been the lengthiest labor of love, but I trust that God will use it as an instrument for giving Him the last word in our lives.

To the courageous ladies who gave God the last word and were willing to share their stories: Lacey, Vanessa, Casia, Josephine*, Sherry, Maryellen, Courtney, Katie, LaNae, Libby, Linda, and Jocelynn.

Katie Forbess, for countless hours on the phone and Skype seeking God's direction for Iron Rose Sister Ministries and this book. You are way more than a glorified cheerleader.

I have not faced any aspect of this process alone. And I would like to specifically thank my parents, David and Jocelynn Goff, for tirelessly walking with me in the process.

George Brown for passing down his knowledge about life, the Bible, and his treasury of quotes and illustrations. I think some of the content of this book may just be on the final exam.

Susan Tolleson, of Propel Book Coaching, for helping me prepare a thorough proposal to submit to publishing companies, for editing several of the chapters in the initial stages, and for your encouragement.

To those who continue to fight these lies and shared their insight about which lies should be included in this book, thank you.

And to others who helped in the editing and revision process: Christa Duve, Erica Peck, Jennifer (Goff) Sale, Carla Sumner, Lois Voyles, and the Tuesday and Wednesday night Bible study groups in my home.

Finally, I am honored to serve with the Iron Rose Sister Ministries (IRSM) Board of Directors and all IRSM Prayer Warriors.

Special thanks to the hosts and hostesses for the multiple writing retreats:

➢ Bob & Eileen Gresham for the use of their cabin for concentrated writing time.
➢ Sherry Hubright for accompanying me on the second writing retreat, not to mention your edits, and your input.
➢ Paxton and Kim (Goff) Edwards for the space in your home and the writing breaks with the kids.
➢ David and Vanessa Gilliam for their hospitality during my final stretch of writing.

Huge thanks to the following specific individuals for the use of their talents:

➢ Katie Lynn Finch for the cover image.
➢ Kenneth Mills for the cover design.
➢ Geoffrey Wyatt for the bio picture.
➢ Joel Friedlander, Book Template Designs.

Names changed per the contributor's request.

Iron Rose Sister Ministries Bible Studies Format

T he Iron Rose Sister Ministries (IRSM) Bible Studies are designed for a small group context. Even if it were possible for me to give you "all the answers" and share my perspective on the verses and concepts being presented, I cannot emphasize enough the value of fellowship, discussion and prayer with other Christian sisters! The format of the IRSM Bible Studies allows for greater discussion, depth of insight and unique perspectives. If you don't follow the book exactly, that's ok! I invite you to make the studies your own, to allow the Spirit to lead, and to treat the studies as a guide and a resource, not a formula.

The IRSM Bible Studies also provide the opportunity for spiritual journaling on a personal level. I encourage you to date the chapters and add notes in the margins in addition to answering the questions. The 'Common Threads' will also allow you to chronicle your personal growth individually and in communion with your Iron Rose Sisters.

Using the image of the rose and the IRSM logo, the bloom of the rose represents areas we come to recognize in which we long to grow. Through these studies, we can also identify thorns we'd like to work on removing or need help to remove. They may be thorns like Paul's (2 Cor. 12:7-10), but by identifying them; we can know where they are and either dull them or stop sticking others and ourselves with them. The final Common Thread is the iron, which is best defined and facilitated in communion with other Christian sisters, Iron Rose Sisters.

Common Threads in IRSM Studies

how you'd like to grow and bloom

a thorn you'd like to remove

an area in which you are striving to dig deeper or need to have someone hold you accountable

What is an Iron Rose Sister?

An Iron Rose Sister is a Christian sister who serves as iron sharpening iron (Prov. 27:17), encouraging and inspiring others to be as beautiful as a rose in spite of a few thorns.

Purposes of Iron Rose Sister Relationships:

➢ Encouragement and inspiration
➢ Prayer
➢ Understanding and affirmation
➢ Confidentiality
➢ Spiritual audit (IRS)
➢ Mutual call to holy living
➢ Spiritual friendship and conversation

Recommendations for Iron Rose Sister Ministries Bible Studies:

➤ Allow for at least an hour and a half meeting time weekly.
  - o We're women—we like to talk!
  - o Prayer time
  - o Depth of conversation and discussion
➤ Rotate leading the discussion among EACH of the women.
  - o Everyone can lead!
  - o Everyone will grow!
  - o For additional suggestions, see the *Leader's Guide* (pg. vii-viii)
➤ Commit to reading the chapter ahead of time.
  - o The discussion will be richer and deeper if everyone comes prepared.
  - o How much you put in will be directly proportional to how much you get out.
  - o You will need to do these studies with your favorite Bible in hand.
  - o All verses, unless otherwise noted, are quoted from the New International Version (NIV).
➤ Follow up with each other during the week.
  - o Prayer
  - o Encouragement
  - o 'Common Threads'

The IRSM logo designation is used to highlight questions that lend themselves to good group discussion: icebreakers, questions for depth of insight or additional perspectives, and areas for growth and sharing.

Leader's Guide

As presented in the *Iron Rose Sister Ministries Bible Studies Format*, the group is encouraged to rotate who leads the discussion each week.

Even if you do not feel equipped to lead or feel that you lack adequate experience to do so, it is a rich opportunity for growth and blessing. You are among sisters and friends that are supporting you in this part of your journey, as well.

Tips or reminders, especially for new leaders:

➢ Make it your own and allow the Spirit to lead—these studies are a resource, not a script.
  ○ Select which questions you would like to discuss, and plan for ones you might need to skip if you are running short on time.
  ○ You are welcome to add questions of your own or highlight portions of the chapter that most stood out to you, whether they were designated for discussion or not.
➢ Leading is about facilitating the discussion, not about having all the answers.
  ○ When someone brings up a difficult situation or challenging question, you can always open it up to the group for answers from Scripture, not just personal advice.

o The answer may merit further Bible study or the consultation of someone with more experience in the Word and/or experience regarding that type of situation. That's okay! We're digging deeper.

➤ Be willing to answer the designated discussion questions first, using your own examples, but avoid the temptation to do all the talking.

o Allow for awkward silence in order to provide the opportunity for others to share.

o It's okay to call on someone and encourage them to answer a specific question.

o "Why or why not?" or "Can you add to that comment?" are good follow-up questions for discussion.

➤ Include additional examples from Scripture and encourage others to do the same.

o Online Bible programs such as BibleGateway.com provide excellent resources like multiple versions of the Bible, concordances (to look up the occurrences of a word), Bible dictionaries, and commentaries.

➤ Give a practical wrap-up conclusion or "take-home" application from the week as you close with the Common Threads.

➤ Be sure to budget some time for prayer.

➤ Remember our purposes as students of the Word and daughters of the King. We are striving to deepen our relationships with God and one another—to be Iron Rose Sisters that serve as iron sharpening iron as we encourage and inspire one another to be as beautiful as a rose in spite of a few thorns.

Preface

Remembering the truth allows God to have the last Word—not our fears, not the lies, not the pain, nor the despair. The truth of God's Word cuts through lies like nothing else.

It is my goal with this book to paint a picture with my words, share a story that inspires, and quote a scripture that breathes truth and hope into a shattered life, battered by lies. These will not exclusively be my stories told on the pages of this interactive Bible study. The timeless tales come from the Bible—powerful messages that transform our lives and fill us with hope. The other testimonies in each chapter come from the lives of women willing to impart some of the wisdom and truth gleaned from the dark days of their soul—lessons learned and verses clung to as they wrestled through Satan's personal attacks and came to own powerful truths found in God's Word.

In *Who Has the Last Word?* you will walk with these women through the entrapping lies into the freedom of truth. And you will explore the truths of Scripture as the Word of God breathes faith, hope, and love in abundance into your lungs, filling you with new life in Christ.

All other things shall cease, but these three remain: faith, hope, and love; and the greatest of these is love (1 Cor. 13:13).

When we embrace truth, we abound in faith, hope, and love—the abundant life that Jesus offers (John 10, 1 Cor. 13, 1 Thes. 1:2-

3, Rom. 5:1-8, 2 Pet. 1:2). Satan came to steal, kill, and destroy, but God sent His Son that we might have an abundant life (John 10:10, *paraphrased*).

I want to point you to the God of Scripture. It is *His* Word. Christ is the embodiment of that Word—the way, the truth and the life (John 14:6)—and we have been given the Spirit of truth, the Holy Spirit, as a continual testimony of that truth.

It is a love story. It is a redemption song. It is filled with poetry, prose, history, genealogy, commands, promises, and vivid descriptions of a loving God relentlessly pursuing a relationship with us.

Many authors have presented well-written, authoritative works on the power of the Word and the influence of Satan's lies. However, I pray that through the format of interactive small group discussion and through the guided study questions, you will gain your own new depth of understanding and appreciation for God's Word and its power in your life.

Who Has the Last Word? encapsulates the primary goal of Iron Rose Sister Ministries: to equip women with the tools to connect to God and one another more deeply. Specifically in this book, I want to equip you with the tools to be practiced wielders of the Word, to fight the lies, and be filled with joy in the abundant life of faith, hope, and love through the transforming power of the truth of God's Word. This is best accomplished in the combined contexts of personal study and small group discussion.

Iron Rose Sister Ministries strives to equip, inspire, and empower women to fight the good fight, finish the race, and rejoice in the crown that awaits them. It is our prayer that your

Iron Rose Sisters will accompany you in this battle, run with you in this race, and cheer you on to victory.

Even if we wanted to attack all the lies with which Satan attacks us, it would be impossible. However, we can look at foundational truths on which we stand (yes, they exist!), the examples of Christ and others who fought Satan's lies with the truth, and proceed with a foundation of faith, hope, and love. We will look at some of the personal lies that overshadow deeper truths and learn how to respond to them. We will address the fear that accompanies the lies and the hope that can shatter it.

As will be highlighted through the Common Threads, the lies of Satan are like deep thorns we are asking God to remove. They are distorted versions of reality that have us entangled and bring us pain.

And through the Lie/Truth Charts, we will begin to recognize the lie, replace the lie with truth, and remember the truth—thus giving God the last word and cutting through Satan's lies with the power of God's Word.

Introduction:
Opening Statement

As a part of my civic duty and in fulfillment of a jury summons, I spent a full day at the local courthouse, most of it in courtroom 406 where a judge explained the judicial process, defined legal terms, and asked pertinent questions of the jury pool after reading the charges for the accused. It was a complicated criminal trial that would take a full week's service.

I was later dismissed and left with the curiosity of how the trial would end, but relieved to not have to spend a week in court weighing the facts and determining, based on those facts, the guilt or innocence of the accused.

I have always been fascinated by crime shows and mysteries—ones that I can watch at a distance and that don't hit too close to home. However, as a different judge mentioned that morning, "If you've ever watched Law & Order[1], they don't show this part on TV because it is boring and there's nothing we can do about it." He was right. But I found myself not bored, but rather intrigued by things I observed that day.

While the judge in courtroom 406 reminded everyone of the judicial process and the attorneys asked their probing questions of

---

[1] National Broadcasting Network

the potential jurors, what most caught my attention was **the number of times someone referred to truth and lies.**

The question was asked: How do you determine if someone is telling the truth? Can you trust the testimony of someone that has a prior conviction? What if someone changes their story? What about their body language might indicate that they are telling the truth or not?

These and many others are valid questions that are not faced exclusively in a courtroom. In our own heads, we serve as judge and jury every time a thought crosses our mind. We must discern whether the thought is a lie or truth, then act accordingly. Just like the little angel and the little devil on each shoulder in many cartoons, we have competing ideas, which go to war and can steal our peace.

Satan has always been quite adept at convincing us that a lie is truth. He works his wiles and devises his schemes to distort truth and introduce doubt. **The good news is that Satan does not have the last word.**

In a courtroom, the judge has the final say in the verdict. He helps the jury judiciously arrive at truth. **In life, Jesus is our Advocate, our Mediator—the One who has the final word.**

Who has the last word in your life? I invite you to join with me and other Christian sisters as we explore these chapters together and cut through Satan's lies with the truth of God's Word.

We will learn to recognize the lie, replace it with truth, and remember that truth when attacked. We will learn tools to help us remember those truths by creating Lie/Truth Charts, through the Common Threads, and by hiding His Word in our hearts.

Are you ready to live the abundant life of faith, hope, and love that God promises? Let's get started!

CHAPTER 1

Recognize, Replace, Remember: The Power of Truth Transforms

The most terrible of lies is not that which is uttered but that which is lived. – W. G. Clarke

I beg your pardon, I didn't recognize you – I've changed a lot. – Oscar Wilde

I can imagine that Peter was reminded of his betrayal every time a rooster crowed. Satan would've made sure of that. Satan wants to capitalize on any lie that hinders us from a life of truth, the abundant life that we are promised—even if it means using a farm bird to do his dirty work. The deceiver longs to ensnare, entrap, and undermine. So every time Peter heard that familiar "cock-a-doodle-doo," he had to cling to words of truth— words of forgiveness and promise—all words of God that strengthened his faith, restored his hope, and bathed him in love.

Peter had a choice after the rooster crowed. He could believe the lie that his identity was that of a betrayer of Jesus. Or he could recognize that it was a lie, replace that lie with the truth of Christ's forgiveness, and move forward, choosing to remember the truth of the abundant life the Messiah had called him to lead.

Had Peter betrayed Jesus? Yes. But was his identity as the betrayer of Jesus accurate? No! He remembered Jesus' words of truth that called him to a life beyond his betrayal, and chose to believe those, instead.

"But I have prayed for you, Simon, that your faith may not fail. And when you have turned back, strengthen your brothers" (Luke 22:32). I believe Simon Peter clung to these and other loving words from Jesus after hearing the rooster crow. They were sorely needed— and welcomed—after having betrayed the one who spoke these words of hope to him. Jesus' truth-filled words invited Peter to be free of the lies that threatened to become a stronghold in his life (Luke 22:31-34, 54-62) and instead, offered an abundant life of faith, hope, and love in Christ.

Simon Peter gave Jesus the last word. He allowed truth to cut through the lies. And he was transformed by the power of the truth in his life.

Who Has the Last Word in Your Life?

Through the course of this interactive Bible study, you will have the opportunity to recognize lies from Satan, replace those lies with truth, and remember the truth when lies threaten to become a stronghold or define your identity. You will have the opportunity to give the life-giver Jesus the last word in your life, not the father of lies.

Each week, you will study the chapter on your own, and then gather with other sisters in Christ to further deepen and broaden the application of these lessons in the context of community. We have so much to offer each other on the journey of transformation from lies to truth as we reclaim the abundant life Satan is working to steal. We may not be able to hear the audible voice of God, but He lovingly speaks the truths found in His Word.

Just as Simon Peter likely had to remind himself of those truths every time a rooster crowed, claiming truth in our lives is a process. He underwent a transformation from Simon (meaning "he has heard") to Peter ("the rock," Matt. 16:18). He was transformed from the outspoken disciple, ready to walk on water (Matt. 14:28) and cut off Malchus' ear in Jesus' defense (John 18:10), to the spokesman for the early church (Acts 2).

Accounts of transformation flood the Scriptures:

➤ From timid beauty queen to savior of a nation (Esther: The book of Esther)
➤ From prostitute to rescuer (Rahab: Josh. 2)
➤ From widow and foreigner to prominent woman in the genealogy of Jesus (Ruth: The book of Ruth; Matt. 1:5)
➤ From bitter to redeemed (Mara/Naomi: Ruth 1:3-5, 19-21, 4:14-17)
➤ From Christian-killer to church leader (Saul/Paul: Acts 9, 11, 13-28)

With which of these examples do you most identify? Or is there another biblical example of transformation that parallels the transformation God is bringing about in your life?

Transformation

The Bible is full of stories of transformation. But it is a process. Even Saul, confronted in an instant with the light of truth and voice of God (Acts 9:3-4), had to go through a transformation process, guided by Ananias, and continued throughout his ministry. He verbalized that struggle of transformation in Romans 7:14 – 8:1. In what I affectionately call the tongue-twister passage, Paul put into words the internal wrestling and difficult work of transformation.

Not all transformations are as dramatic as Paul's. My transformations tend to happen in small ways that I recognize after looking back and reflecting on how God worked through a certain situation.

Your transformation process may not be initially visible to others, but God is working to renew and change you, just as He does with every butterfly. Even as an egg, the caterpillar begins to take shape. In the second stage, the caterpillar eats and eats, growing and shedding its outgrown skin four to five times. The third stage is characterized by the most dramatic transformation—metamorphosis. During this stage, the caterpillar builds a chrysalis and within that outer form, all old body parts of the caterpillar are transformed into the body and wings of a beautiful butterfly. As an adult butterfly recently departed from its chrysalis, a final transformation must still take place. The butterfly's wings are soft, wet, and weak. The insect must use its wings to strengthen them and allow a God-designed transformation to take place so it can fly in beauty, and fulfill the purpose for which it was created.

Just as the butterfly goes through metamorphosis, our transformation to Christlikeness takes time. Maybe at times we catch only a glimpse of what we are to become. There can be pain as we shed the skin of our old selves and the lies that cocooned us. Radical transformation, unseen by many, takes place in our hearts and minds as we continue to work and allow God to transform us into strong and beautiful creations that rest and thrive in the abundant life He has designed for us.

Journey of Transformation

On our journey of transformation through this book, you will be asked to look up verses, answer questions, think through your answers, and discover truths for yourself and about yourself. We remember and own those truths as we go through the process of learning them—not by permitting someone else to spoon-feed them to us.

If you don't feel as though you have all of the answers, don't get discouraged! None of us have all the answers. **Transformation is the process of discovering and learning, and a journey we do not travel alone.**

Throughout each chapter, some questions will be highlighted with the logo of Iron Rose Sister Ministries (IRSM).

Let me take a moment to explain what this is all about and why I'm so passionate about it. Nothing is more frustrating as a Christian than the desire to change, to be transformed, and not know how to do it. My goal through this ministry (IRSM) is to provide you, and other women, with the tools to make transformation possible—through the power of the Word—and the opportunity to walk on the journey of transformation with others, because we cannot do it alone.

In brief introduction, IRSM is a bilingual (English and Spanish) women's ministry resource dedicated to equipping, inspiring, and empowering women in their relationships with God and other women. The ministry's name is rooted in the fact that we all want that kind of a Christian sister that can be like iron sharpening iron, encouraging and inspiring us to be as beautiful as a rose in spite of a few thorns—an Iron Rose Sister. For more information about IRSM, visit www.IronRoseSister.com

The IRSM logo also identifies questions you can use for good discussion when you meet with your small group (your Iron Rose Sisters). Here's the first suggested question for discussion in this chapter:

 How does Romans 12:1-2 describe the transformation process?

Where does renewal take place?

Abounding in Faith, Hope, and Love

It is in our mind and heart that Satan works diligently to hinder us from the fulfilling, abundant life God offers. However, through a new life in Christ, we can reclaim those promises. We can abound in faith, hope, and love as we are being transformed into Christlikeness and claim the abundant life He promises in John 10:10.

Let's look at how Romans 5:1-8 describes that transformation-filled promise.

Therefore, since we have been justified through faith, we have peace with God through our Lord Jesus Christ, [2] through whom we have gained access by faith into this grace in which we now stand. And we boast in the hope of the glory of God. [3] Not only so, but we also glory in our sufferings, because we know that suffering produces perseverance; [4] perseverance, character; and character, hope. [5] And hope does not put us to shame, because God's love has been poured out into our hearts through the Holy Spirit, who has been given to us.

[6] You see, at just the right time, when we were still powerless, Christ died for the ungodly. [7] Very rarely will anyone die for a righteous person, though for a good person someone might possibly dare to die. [8] But God demonstrates his own love for us in this: While we were still sinners, Christ died for us.

What kind of abundant life is being offered in Romans 5?

Draw a triangle around the word "faith" every time it occurs in the written-out verses (Rom. 5:1-8). Circle the word "hope" every time it occurs, and draw a heart around the word "love."

 What does highlighting those words bring to light in Romans 5:1-8?

Faith, Hope, and Love Defined

Faith, hope, and love are foundational to our transformation and embracing of truth. The most familiar reference to faith, hope, and love is found in 1 Corinthians 13, where Paul also tells us that all other things shall cease... "And now these three remain: faith, hope, and love. But the greatest of these is love" (1 Cor. 13:13).

Read the following verses describing faith, hope, and love. Allow God's guidance and promises to wash over you. Then describe what an abundant life, transformed by these qualities, would look like.

 Faith – Matthew 17:20; Romans 10:17; Hebrews 11:6

 Hope – Romans 8:24-25, 15:13; Hebrews 6:19

 Love – Philippians 1:9; Romans 8:35-39; John 15:9

Faith, hope, and love are not as the world would define them. Throughout the Sermon on the Mount, Jesus offered a new and better definition of those promises—and so many other misunderstood concepts—about His Father, the kingdom, and God's teachings. Jesus' message was based on replacing lies with truths. "You have heard that it is said… but I tell you…"

Starting with the Beatitudes, Jesus turned His hearers' world upside down. What the world presented as truth, He revealed as a lie. We are going to look at a few select passages from Matthew 5-7 to illustrate Jesus' desire to reveal the distorted truths as the lies they were, then to replace them with His words of truth.

Using the verses quoted from the book of Matthew in the chart below, and Jesus' example of how to give God the last word, take a moment to fill in the following Lie/Truth Chart.

We will use the format of this chart as a pattern for recognizing the lies, replacing lies with truth, and remembering the truth in subsequent chapters. I have done the first row for you.

Please put these lies and truths in your own words—make them personal so they can begin to soak into you, and God can work His transformation. And when you gather with your Iron Rose Sisters, you'll notice that Satan twists his lies in different ways for each of us—all lies, but one truth.

RECOGNIZE the lie (in your own words)	REPLACE the lie with truth (in your own words)	REMEMBER the truth (biblical reference)
Admitting my spiritual weakness means I will get trampled by others or seen as a failing Christian.	By admitting my spiritual need, I am promised heaven!	"Blessed are the poor in spirit, for theirs is the kingdom of heaven." Matt. 5:3

RECOGNIZE	REPLACE	REMEMBER
		"You have heard that it was said, 'Love your neighbor and hate your enemy.' But I tell you, love your enemies and pray for those who persecute you." **Matt. 5:43-44**
		"Do not store up for yourselves treasures on earth, where moths and vermin destroy, and where thieves break in and steal. But store up for yourselves treasures in heaven... For where your treasure is, there your heart will be also." **Matt. 6:19-21**
		"Not everyone who says to me, 'Lord, Lord,' will enter the kingdom of heaven, but only the one who does the will of my Father who is in heaven." **Matt. 7:21**

After recognizing these lies and replacing them with truth, each stated in your own words, what do you notice about the abundant life offered in Christ?

How do faith, hope, and love help us realize the transformation we desire, recognizing, replacing, and remembering in our process of transformation?

Faith:

Hope:

Love:

Our Transformational Journey through *Who Has the Last Word?*

In chapters 2-5 of *Who Has the Last Word?* we will explore the transforming power of the Word, hidden in our heart, as well as the importance of each of the steps: to recognize the lie, replace it with truth, and remember the truth.

In chapters 6-13 of this book, you have the opportunity to fill in a Lie/Truth Chart that speaks to the lies presented in the chapter, and the specific lies with which Satan attacks you personally. The Lie/Truth Chart is also designed to give you at least one specific scriptural reference to remind you of the truth, as well as that truth put in your own words.

The back of the book has a large, blank Lie/Truth Chart (pg. 293) for you to fill in with truths that resonate with you as you read the book. You can later detach that page and put it in a familiar place for easy reference when you are being attacked by Satan's lies. (Also available for download on our website: www.IronRoseSister.com)

Each week, try to take at least one truth (or one verse) and write it on a notecard that you can post on your mirror or in the kitchen—someplace you'll see it daily. You can also make a note in your phone. These memory tools are practical ways to allow God's truths to sink into your heart and mind, and to renew your identity in Christ.

You don't need to feel intimidated by those who know their Bible better than you, or those who can quote book, chapter, and verse. We are all in this together, and with more practice and time in the Word, we will grow in our ability to remember the truth and live by it.

As we proceed on this transformational journey together, I would like to encourage you with a few tips for Bible reading:

➢ Reference multiple versions of the Bible. While we all have our favorite version, reading another version can expand our understanding of the Bible. Some versions are focused on a word-by-word translation and others have a thought-by-thought approach. Each has its merits as the living and active sword which expresses the truth you need to hear in a way that resonates anew and cuts through the lies you are fighting.

➢ Online Bible resources are a wonderful way to access multiple versions while providing an easy search engine as a concordance:

- o www.BibleGateway.com
- o www.BlueLetterBible.org
- o www.Bible.com
- o Each of these sites also has a mobile version (for iPhone, Android, iPad, tablet, etc.)

➢ Become familiar with the practice of using a concordance: a list of occurrences of a word or phrase found in Scripture. Many printed Bibles have a small concordance in the back. Concordances help us cross-reference a particular word or topic across the entire content of the Bible, but I encourage you to look at the verse in context, not just the single verse on its own.

➢ Footnotes are not found in some online Bibles, but in printed Bibles, or when included online, they serve to reference the scripture quoted in the text. We will look at several footnotes in chapter 2, "I Have Hidden Your Word in My Heart," as Jesus quotes the Old Testament in response to Satan.

One of my prayers in preparing this study is that you will come to know the truth of the Word and the transforming power it has in our lives. I pray you will become more familiar with the Bible and tap into its strength when you feel attacked by Satan's lies.

Common Threads

We will close this chapter as we close each chapter, with the Common Threads. They represent the three parts of the Iron Rose Sister Ministries logo, and have a special application for lies and truth. The Common Threads are a way to make each lesson personal and practical while offering the opportunity to pray over each other in a small group setting.

The Common Threads are also a tool by which you can grow in your spiritual friendships as Iron Rose Sisters—to be that iron sharpening iron as we encourage and inspire each other to be as beautiful as a rose in spite of a few thorns. By walking on this spiritual journey of transformation together with other Christian women, I invite you to learn what it really means to have an accountability partner, a prayer partner, and a Christian friend: an Iron Rose Sister.

In addition to the Common Threads serving as a tool for prayer, accountability, and personal application, each chapter is dated so it can serve as a form of spiritual journaling. I pray you will later look back and rejoice in your growth.

Your Common Threads this week may come from the comparative look of lies and truth from the Sermon on the Mount, or from the concept of transformation. I encourage you to spend some time in prayer as you consider the ways in which God is already walking with you to recognize the lies, replace the lies with truth, and remember the truth. When you meet as a group, be sure to set aside some time to share your Common Threads with each other.

 An area in which you'd like to grow or bloom—abounding in faith, hope, and love through truth.

_____

_____

A thorn (lie) you'd like to remove and replace with truth.

_____

_____

An area in which you'd like to dig deeper or need someone to hold you accountable (help to recognize the lie or remember the truth).

_____

_____

A verse or truth to remember that speaks to a lie mentioned in this chapter.

_____

_____

We have already covered a lot in this first chapter! Thank you for joining in this transformational journey, made possible by the power of the Word. May God bless you with the abundant life of faith, hope, and love, by recognizing the lie, replacing the lie with truth, and remembering the truth. The power of truth transforms—and God is inviting you to embrace that transformation and give Him the last word.

CHAPTER 2

I Have Hidden Your Word in My Heart

The longer you read the Bible, the more you will like it; it will grow sweeter and sweeter; and the more you get into the spirit of it, the more you will get into the spirit of Christ. – Romaine

With a word, God spoke the world into existence. And with a word, Jesus healed the royal official's son and the royal official "took Jesus at his word" (John 4:50).

With a word, Peter betrayed his Lord. But later, he transformed his words, preaching a Spirit-led sermon on the day of Pentecost, and affirming, along with John that "we cannot help speaking about what we have seen and heard" (Acts 4:20).

Moses did not think himself capable of eloquent words, yet God used him to declare to Pharaoh the freeing words of promise for God's people, "Let my people go" (Ex. 5:1).

Words are powerful. Words have brokered peace and have started wars. Words can start a relationship, and can end it just as quickly. Words can affirm or destroy, build up or tear down, empower or imprison.

Words may not be written in stone, but they are written on our hearts in a way that shape who we are, guide what we do, and direct decisions we make.

What words are you listening to? Even more importantly, *whose* words are you listening to?

Just as in the cartoons, we deliberate over which voice to listen to: The little devil or the little angel; the lie or the truth. We deliberate like a jury deciding a verdict, weighing the evidence, and listening to the arguments on each side.

Who are you giving the last word? Who has the closing argument on the thoughts that swirl in your mind and threaten to overtake you?

Thankfully, we have Christ as our mediator **and** our advocate (1 Tim. 2:5). Jesus is the best attorney to present the closing argument and voice truth, not only in our defense before the Father, but also as we battle the lies in our minds. I invite you to keep Him and His Father's Word hidden in your heart so that He has the final word. Through Christ, who *is* the Word (John 1), we can recognize the lies, replace them with truth, and remember the truth, thus claiming the abundant life He offers.

> *In the beginning was the Word and the Word was with God and the Word was God. In him was life, and that life was the light of all mankind. The light shines in the darkness, and the darkness has not overcome it. The true light that gives light to everyone was coming into the world. The Word became flesh and made his dwelling among us. We have seen his glory, the glory of the one and only Son, who came from the Father, full of grace and truth.* (John 1:1, 4-5, 14)

The Word came full of grace and truth. As life and light, the Word was full of power to conquer death and crush Satan. **The Word became flesh and was the final answer and closing argument to all of our internal struggles and debates.**

We have access to that power, grace, and truth through a life in Christ. What a promise! We also are reminded of those truths through God's written Word, the Bible.

Tapping into the Power of the Word

Psalm 119 is a poetic declaration by the shepherd David of the beauty and power of God's Word. It is the longest chapter of the Bible, rich with language that reminds us of the Word's transforming nature when put into practice.

Use Psalm 119 as your personal devotional time this week, meditating on the ways in which David highlights the merits of the Word. He asks God to replace his own lies with truth from the Word—what a powerful example!

Throughout the chapter, David uses many synonyms to describe God's Word. In verses 1-12, we see at least eight distinct references to the Word.

For the following exercise:

- ➢ Read Psalm 119:1-12 and list below, in the first column, the description of the Word.
- ➢ In the second column, explain what that description means, or implies about the Word.
- ➢ When you gather in your small group (with your Iron Rose Sisters), your lists may not match exactly if you are using different versions of the Bible. What a great opportunity to glean yet another perspective on the Word!

> Feel free to use a dictionary to understand the different nuances of each description.

Description of the Word	What that description means or implies
Law of the Lord	An established guideline we should obey
Statutes	

 What do the above descriptions imply about the role of the Word in our lives today?

Isn't it amazing to reflect on how the Bible can apply to so many different areas of our lives?! Jesus knew and drew on that power when He was attacked and tempted by Satan. Christ provided a perfect model of how to combat Satan's attacks and cut through the lies that tempt us to fall, hinder us from the abundant life, or distract us from abounding in the faith, hope, and love that God offers each of us.

How Jesus Used the Word When He Was Tempted

Let's look at the temptation of Jesus as a model for fighting Satan's lies—the same pattern we will follow throughout the book. Read Matthew 4:1-11.

Satan capitalizes on our weaknesses. What is the weakness that Satan exploits in the first temptation (Matt. 4:2-3)?

The easiest lie to believe is the one that has an element of truth. What is the truthful portion of what Satan says in verse 3?

Did Jesus have the power to turn the stones to bread?

 Would there have been anything wrong with turning stones to bread? Why or why not?

How did Jesus answer Satan?

Where is that verse found? (You can often refer to a footnote in your Bible for the scriptural reference.)

What is the significance of the verse that man does not live by bread alone? What does it mean to live on every word that comes from the mouth of God?

Let's move on to the second temptation. With what does Satan tempt Jesus?

What does Satan quote?

Did you catch that?! Satan himself quoted the Scriptures!

How are we to discern which scripture to obey if it seems, as it does in the second temptation, that they are in conflict?

Consider the Source

How did Jesus discern? He considered the source. When I started middle school, I transitioned from a private Christian school, where I went from kindergarten through fifth grade, to a magnet school in downtown Baton Rouge, Louisiana. It was the late 1980s, so there was a lot of talk about sex, drugs, and rock 'n roll. Music videos and subliminal messages were becoming more popular and the sexual aspects of that influence will be discussed in the Sexual Lies chapter (ch. 12). From my innocent and sheltered perspective, I thought not only that all the kids I rode on the bus with were with going to hell, but that I was going too, just for breathing the same air as they!

Needless to say, I was facing culture shock, and felt it was obvious to all of the other students that I did not quite fit in. The pre-teen years of middle school are a challenge to navigate even when you don't make this kind of transition. The new world of hormones and self-discovery are thrown into the mix of a lot of life lessons to learn—and don't forget the schoolwork and studies!

As part of my personal adjustment, I was unsure how to handle the bullying jeers from other kids. I usually could just brush it off and ignore their taunts, but at times, the sting was deep and the pain was real.

I remember on one such occasion, I asked my mom for advice on how to handle it. I was beginning to believe their lies and feel the weight of their negativity. She told me to "consider the source." Were these cut-downs and critiques coming from someone who loved me and wanted what was best for me, or from classmates unsure of themselves and seeking to puff up themselves by putting me down?

Please don't hear me saying that my middle-school classmates were evil incarnate. However, I do believe that their attacks were similar to Satan's, and so it is *always* wise to consider the source.

In Matthew 4:7, Jesus recognized that Satan's words were a test—a distorted truth intended to trap Him. How did He answer Satan in verse 7?

Where do we find the original scripture Jesus quoted?

Not only did Jesus consider the source, but He clung to the greater truths of Scripture that could not be overshadowed by taking a verse out of context or, as some of my Southern friends have said, by "picking a pig path through the Bible" (finding portions of verses, taken out of context, to prove a point).

In the third temptation, we see Jesus going to the most basic teaching of God and shutting Satan up with that truth. Reread verses 8-11 of Matthew 4.

How does Satan taunt and test Jesus here?

How does Jesus respond? (Be sure to include the biblical reference of the verse Jesus quotes.)

Let's turn to Deuteronomy 6 and read verses 4-9. What challenge is issued to the Israelites, which is also an important reminder for today?

Where else do we see the teaching in Deuteronomy 6—the same teaching with which Jesus answered Satan?

Considering Jesus' response mirrors the first two of the Ten Commandments (Ex. 20:3-6), and the first of the Greatest Commands (Matt. 22:37-38), what do we learn about how to respond to Satan's attacks?

The Greater Truths

There are foundational truths and commands that cannot be shaken. I would even call them "greater truths" that Jesus was able to trust and rely on, in order to put Satan in his place.

One time a music teacher was visited by an old friend who asked him what good news he had for him today. The old teacher was silent as he stood up and walked across the room, picked up a hammer, and struck a tuning fork. As the note sounded out through the room, he said, "That is *A*. It is *A* today; it was *A* five thousand years ago, and it will be *A* ten thousand years from now. The soprano upstairs sings off-key, the tenor across the hall flats on his high notes, and the piano downstairs is out of tune." He struck the note again and said, "That is *A*, my friend, and that's the good news for today."

Our God is the same yesterday, today, and forever (Heb. 13:8). "For the Lord is good and his love endures forever; his faithfulness continues through all generations" (Ps. 100:5). And that, my friends, is the good news for today!

 What is a go-to verse you can lean on to remind you of the eternal truths about God? List three verses that hold promise for you and that you have hidden in your heart. If you don't know the biblical reference, this is a great opportunity to use a concordance.

These are foundational truths on which we can rely—truths that root our faith when the storms of life prevail.

I encourage you to delight in the Word as David did and spend time in God's Word as a way of knowing Him more personally, completely, and deeply. It will strengthen your faith, fill you with hope, and wash you anew with God's love.

In the same way that Jesus did in the desert when tempted, we can lean on foundational truths found in the Bible as a basis for our faith. These truths are an excellent tool for combatting the lies Satan whispers in our moments of weakness.

May we be rooted and established in these foundational truths—not to convince others of our point of view or enter into doctrinal debates—that is not the purpose of this book. Rather, it is to fall more in love with God through the transforming power of His Word. And by so doing, we will abound in faith, hope, and love, and be better prepared for Satan's attacks.

I would like to echo Paul's prayer over the Ephesians as my prayer over you through your reading and study of *Who Has the Last Word?*

I pray that out of his glorious riches he may strengthen you with power through his Spirit in your inner being, so that Christ may dwell in your hearts through faith. And I pray that you, being rooted and established in love, may have power, together with all the Lord's holy people, to grasp how wide and long and high and deep is the love of Christ, and to know this love that surpasses knowledge— that you may be filled to the measure of all the fullness of God. (Eph. 3:16-19)

Common Threads

You may not have a clear answer to all of the Common Threads at this point, but I encourage you to pray over them. Some of them may come to light after your time in group discussion with your Iron Rose Sisters small group. And don't forget to date the chapters, so that you can look back later and see the growth (a form of spiritual journaling).

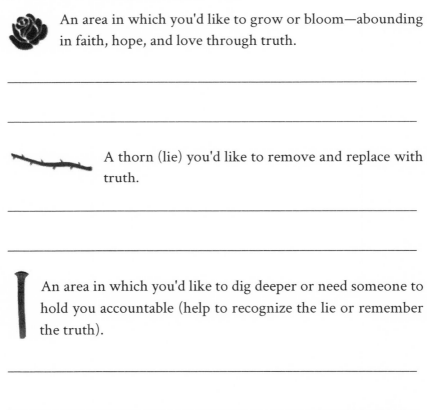

An area in which you'd like to grow or bloom—abounding in faith, hope, and love through truth.

_____

_____

A thorn (lie) you'd like to remove and replace with truth.

_____

_____

An area in which you'd like to dig deeper or need someone to hold you accountable (help to recognize the lie or remember the truth).

_____

_____

A verse or truth to remember that speaks to a lie mentioned in this chapter.

_____

_____

CHAPTER 3

Recognize the Lie

A little lie is like a little pregnancy—it doesn't take long before everyone knows.
– C.S. Lewis

Sin has many tools, but a lie is the handle which fits them all. – Edmund Burke

The easiest person to deceive is one's self. – Unknown

You can rob a bank with a toy gun because someone believes the lie. And while I am not advocating this practice, I am in awe of its reality. Ignoring the fact that robbing a bank is a wrong and illegal action, it seems ridiculous that someone would endeavor to do so using a toy gun. But which is the bigger fool: the robber using a toy gun or the banker that believes the lie and hands over the money?

A lie is only powerful inasmuch as we believe it and act on it. If the banker had been familiar with guns, maybe even owned a gun of his own, he might have readily recognized the fake and not become paralyzed by fear.

We are best able to recognize the lie when we are familiar with the truth.

Note: While the focus of this chapter is recognizing the lie, remember that it is only the first step in the transformation process. Chapters 4 and 5 will walk us through how to Replace the Lie and Remember the Truth.

The FBI and Department of Treasurer workers, when training their agents in the counterfeit department, spend all of their time studying, touching, and smelling all of the details of the true bills. They do not look at *any* counterfeit bills. Why do you think that is?

God longs to demonstrate genuine faith, hope, and love so that we can immediately recognize the false manifestations of those qualities of an abundant life. Satan "masquerades as an angel of light" (2 Cor. 11:14), and his goal is that of a thief: to steal, kill, and destroy (John 10:10a). He is using a toy gun, a weak tool that, when exposed, crumbles and, once out of the way, allows us to have life, and have it to the full in Christ (John 10:10b).

Let's explore a few more verses about Satan as we strive to understand the enemy we are up against and put him in his place. As you read each of the following verses, write down the descriptions of Satan and his schemes.

John 8:44

Mark 4:1-20 (verse 15)

1 Peter 5:8

Genesis 3:1

 Looking at all of these descriptions of the devil, how does Satan undermine the truth?

 Why does Satan want to undermine the truth?

Satan's Early Schemes

Let's take it all the way back to the beginning with the first deception in Genesis 3. Your Bible may still be opened there, so let's read the entire account, verses 1-13.

How does the serpent start his attack in verse 1?

How does Eve respond to the doubt that has been introduced?

 How does the serpent ensnare Eve with deception in Genesis 3:4-5 (refer also to verse 22)?

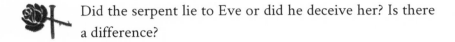 It has been said that the easiest lie to believe is the one that has an element of truth. Would you agree with that statement? Why or why not?

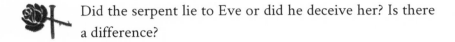 Did the serpent lie to Eve or did he deceive her? Is there a difference?

Either way, Eve had a choice: to trust God and that His commands were for her own good, or be enticed by Satan's lie. God loves us and wants what is best for us. Satan wants to undermine that relationship and tear us apart. When we fall into Satan's deceptive traps and cunning lies, sin enters in and sin separates us from God (Is. 59:1-2).

Read Genesis 3:21-24.

"Man has now become like one of us, knowing good and evil." What does it mean to now know good and evil? What should we do with that knowledge?

Cling to True Faith, Hope, and Love

We must learn to discern between good and evil. However, while we are pursuing clarification and discernment, Satan wants to blur the lines and twist the definitions.

Referring back to Eve in Genesis 3, Satan worked to undermine Eve's faith, offer her false hope, and cause her to forget the depth of love that God had for her and Adam.

How would you describe the faith, hope, and love Eve had in God *before* she ate of the fruit and fell into Satan's entrapping lie?

Faith

Hope

Love

In what ways did Satan undermine the faith, hope, and love Eve had in God?

 Write out a response Eve could have given Satan using the truths of faith, hope, and love she had in God.

Eve had lost her focus. 2 Corinthians 11:3 gives us a similar warning, "But I am afraid that just as Eve was deceived by the serpent's cunning, your minds may somehow be led astray from your sincere and pure devotion to Christ."

We allow Satan's influence to rattle our faith, lose our sight of hope, and lead us to feel unloved. It is easy to get sidetracked or distracted, and thus have a distorted view of truth. We may not recognize it ourselves if left to our own devices. **God has given us His Word and His body, the church, as ways to keep us in check and help reveal those lies that have us entrapped, distracting us from true faith, hope, and love.** However, as James points out, if we don't do anything about the truth we have seen, if we only listen to the Word, we are deceiving ourselves.

Read James 1:22-25.

How is the Word compared to a mirror?

The Word is a Mirror

I cannot read James 1:22-25 without thinking of the following story. I was working for the North Atlanta Church of Christ in Atlanta, Georgia, as Assistant to the Director of Missions. One of my responsibilities was to serve as a liaison to the missionaries supported by that church. I was a recent college grad and was ready to conquer the world. I was working there in preparation to join a team to Bogotá, Colombia, in the near future. Spanish was already my nerdy passion, as I call it, and so I was excited to be a part of church plantings, campaigns, youth camps, and women's retreats in Mexico, Colombia, and Venezuela.

However, the church in Atlanta also supported missionaries in Russia and Kazakhstan. My love of travel pushed me to follow through in those ventures as well, but I admit that in anticipation of the month that I was going to spend in Irkutsk, Russia, I had a bad attitude. I was asking God how He would use me in a place where I didn't know the language or the culture, and where it would be cold! This Louisiana girl had never lived out of the South and the warmer temperatures found there.

I found a great winter coat on sale and was blessed with the gift of some winter boots before departure. My attitude still needed some work, but I relied on one of my favorite verses, "Here am I. Send me!" (Is. 6:8).

The travel time of more than twenty-four hours meant that I remember little about the car tour of Moscow, but somehow the men standing on the wing of the plane breaking the ice in order that we could depart, sticks clearly in my mind. Maybe it was also because I watched this scene unfold while there were more of us crammed into a shuttle bus to get to the plane than clowns can fit in a clown car. We were certainly warmer for those sardine-packed minutes in the bus. We finally arrived at Irkutsk and settled in to recover from jet lag.

One of the ways in which the missionaries were serving and reaching out to the community was by teaching English classes using the Bible. We accompanied them and guest-taught in a class or two—a great opportunity for us to meet people, serve, and spread the gospel.

One of the students I met in the beginners' class was a girl named Yulia. Her very limited English and my non-existent Russian made for broken communication, but I quickly discovered that she was a university student studying, of all things, Spanish! I couldn't believe it and began to laugh at God's sense of humor.

Yulia and I began speaking to each other in Spanish. Yes. A Russian and an American in Irkutsk, Russia, speaking Spanish. I still shake my head at the memory. Yulia and I began to study the Bible together and one afternoon, I was telling her about the Ethiopian eunuch (Acts 8:26-40) and the four things I respected about him. 1) He understood the importance of worshipping God and traveled great distances to do so. 2) He valued the Word of God and read what he could access while on that journey. 3) When he had a question, he asked and God provided Philip to answer those questions. 4) When he understood what he needed to do, he did it right away—was baptized.

Yulia was intrigued and was full of questions herself. I thanked her for her searching spirit and she thanked me for allowing God to use me like Philip to help answer those questions. She proceeded to ask me if I might also be able to answer some questions that her roommate had about God and the Bible. I agreed immediately and we arranged for me to go to their flat (apartment) the following afternoon.

Yulia lived with four other university students and so we tucked ourselves back in one of their bedrooms for a more private study with Yulia and her roommate. I taught in Spanish and Yulia translated from Spanish to Russian. I know that God was smiling at how He was able to use me at that time.

While we were studying, another roommate stumbled in the bedroom door and, with a small glass of clear liquid, asked in slurred Russian, "What are you doing?" Yulia, obviously embarrassed and at a loss for words, simply held up the Bible and sheepishly said, "We're studying the Bible." At this, the roommate who had entered stood straight up; her face went pale; she turned without saying a word and walked out the door.

We were all silent for a moment, absorbing what had just happened. Then Yulia began to apologize to me for her roommate's behavior, clarifying that she, Yulia, doesn't drink like that, and wondering if I was too offended for us to continue our study. I assured Yulia that she had nothing to worry about and nothing to apologize for. "Yulia," I said, "it's okay. **This is just the first time that she has ever seen herself in the mirror of God's Word.**"

Convicted by Scripture

Have you ever been cut to the heart like that? Convicted by what you see in Scripture as God revealed a lie in your life?

Make note of the verse or Bible story that convicted you. Be sure to include details about the events surrounding that moment.

 How did you feel when convicted in that way or when you recognized the lie?

As we expose the lie, there is a certain vulnerability that comes with it.

Lies are Personal

Since we all struggle with different lies, we must be careful to not dismiss the pain and bondage associated with the lies that entrap others or think that they should step right out of it. We are all in this together and God has given us the Great Comforter to validate our pain and walk with us to freedom.

Satan knows how to capitalize on each of our respective weaknesses. I had to come to recognize the lie of Satan that to allow myself to be human meant that I was living according to the flesh, and therefore, was sinning. A study of the life of Jesus freed me from that lie and showed me that I could allow myself to be human, just as He was, and do it in a holy way. If you would like to learn more about that particular lie, be sure to check out the first Iron Rose Sister Ministries study, *Human AND Holy*.

That may not be a lie that you struggle with, but I'm sure that there are others that are very real to you. I have entered that lie with which I struggled, into the Lie/Truth Chart below as an example.

Using the verses of truth in the subsequent rows, fill in a lie that can be recognized in light of that truth. This may or may not be a lie that you wrestle with yourself, but I encourage you to be specific in the ways Satan attacks through that lie. The father of lies and great deceiver does not want to be recognized, but let's take the opportunity to call him out and reveal who he really is through his entrapping lies. Don't forget to replace that lie with truth in your own words.

RECOGNIZE the lie (in your own words)	REPLACE the lie with truth (in your own words)	REMEMBER the truth (biblical reference)
If I allow myself to be human and express the intensity of human emotions I feel, I am living according to the flesh and, therefore, am sinning.	Jesus came in the flesh and faced the same human emotions and human conditions that I face, yet was without sin. Expressing my emotions in a healthy and holy way is not a sin!	"Therefore, since we have a great high priest who has ascended into heaven, Jesus the Son of God, let us hold firmly to the faith we profess. For we do not have a high priest who is unable to empathize with our weaknesses, but we have one who has been tempted in every way, just as we are—yet he did not sin. Let us then approach God's throne of grace with confidence, so that we may receive mercy and find grace to help us in our time of need." Heb. 4:14-16
		"For no matter how many promises God has made, they are "Yes" in Christ. And so through him the "Amen" is spoken by

		us to the glory of God." **2 Cor. 1:20**
		"The Lord appeared to us in the past, saying: "I have loved you with an everlasting love; I have drawn you with unfailing kindness. Then young women will dance and be glad, young men and old as well. I will turn their mourning into gladness; I will give them comfort and joy instead of sorrow." **Jer. 31:3, 13**

 What aspects of faith, hope, and love do you see in the truths listed in the above Lie/Truth Chart?

 When you gather together in your small group of Iron Rose Sisters, share the *Recognize* and *Replace* columns with each other. Notice the uniqueness of each of your answers as Satan works to attack people differently, but the power of the truths we can *Remember* and give God the last word!

List two benefits of writing out the lies and the truth.

Recognize the Lie with Light

Writing out the lies and truth are similar to verbalizing them or confessing our sins. When we confess our sins one to another (James 5:17), some of the power that sin has over us is diminished. In the same way, verbalizing the lie removes some of the weight of its distorted reality. I know that is not an easy step to take, but it is a powerful and vital step. Even if verbalizing the lie to a Christian sister—an Iron Rose Sister who has committed to walking with you on your spiritual journey—is too overwhelming at this point, I encourage you to verbalize it to God. Allow Him to bring it to light and lift that burden from you.

As I mention bringing the lies to light, I want to close with one more set of verses.

What does Paul compare deceit and truth with in Ephesians 5:6-17?

What relationship does Jesus describe between light and truth in John 3:20-21?

We will be unable to recognize the lies until we bring them to the light of the Word. And when exposed, like cockroaches, they will flee!

I pray that through the course of this study, you will be able to recognize some of Satan's lies in your personal life, bring them to light, and reclaim the faith, hope, and love that we have in God and that Satan has stolen in the process.

Let's recognize the lies and give God the last word in those specific areas!

Common Threads

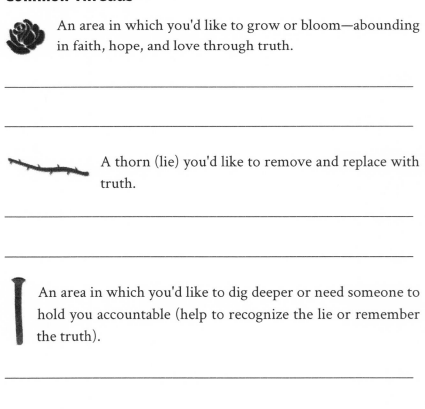

An area in which you'd like to grow or bloom—abounding in faith, hope, and love through truth.

_____

_____

A thorn (lie) you'd like to remove and replace with truth.

_____

_____

An area in which you'd like to dig deeper or need someone to hold you accountable (help to recognize the lie or remember the truth).

_____

_____

A verse or truth to remember that speaks to a lie mentioned in this chapter.

CHAPTER 4

Replace the Lie with Truth

The truth is always the strongest argument. – Sophocles

Finding out the truth is only half of it. It's what you do with it that matters. – Zach, The Secret Life of Bees[2]

To recognize the lie is only the first step. Vitally important is the next step: Replacing the lie with truth. I think we each wish this would happen in an immediate fashion—like downing an energy drink and getting a rush of spiritual adrenaline every time we read or study the Bible. That spiritual jolt may hit us occasionally, but the benefits of the Word of God are more like taking your vitamins or eating your vegetables. People who take their vitamins and eat their vegetables do so because of the long-term benefit, not because every time they eat their spinach, they suddenly develop huge muscles like Popeye. Over the long haul, taking vitamins and eating vegetables are going to have a beneficial effect on physical health, resistance to disease, and general wellbeing.

---

[2] Fox Searchlight Pictures, 2008.

The same is true of reading the Bible. At times, it will have a sudden impact on us, like it did Yulia's roommate in the story I shared in chapter 3. However, the real value lies in the cumulative effects that long-term exposure to God's Word will bring to our lives: a true transformation. **We will slowly and consistently replace lies with truth in such a way that the truth becomes a part of who we are and how we identify ourselves: a beloved child of God.**

What happens when we are focused on the lie? Allow me to provide an illustration: It's the New Year and you have decided to join your friend at the gym and in a diet that eliminates all sugar for the first thirty days. No problem, right? Yeah, right! It's now January 8th and your sister has a birthday. All you can think about is her favorite chocolate cake that will be at the party. You become consumed by the chocolate cake. All your thoughts are focused on the chocolate cake. The party is tomorrow and your ability to maintain your resolve for the diet with your friend is wavering. I mean, it's chocolate cake!

So, you decide that you can conquer this temptation. "I am not going to think about the chocolate cake. I'm not going to think about the chocolate cake. I am NOT going to think about the chocolate cake." What is the only thing you are thinking about? Yep. The chocolate cake.

You have to *replace* the thoughts about chocolate cake with something else: "I'm going to bring a sugar-free chocolate bar with me and focus on the blessing of time with family." Problem solved? Not for all eternity, but maybe for the birthday party and today's temptation.

Replacing the Lie with Truth

 What happens when we do not replace a lie with truth?

Matthew 12:43-45 paints a picture of the importance of replacing a lie with truth. What does Jesus describe in these verses?

What made the man's final condition worse than the first?

How could that have been avoided?

 Would it be fair to describe a lie that has taken hold and become part of our identity as a stronghold? Describe a stronghold, allowing yourself to reflect on a specific stronghold in your own life.

As we discussed in chapter 3, we have to walk with God, in the light of His Word, to reveal and recognize those lies and strongholds. We may not know what they are yet and, if you don't, do not be discouraged. We will work together to recognize them and replace them with truth!

It is a spiritual battle to demolish the strongholds. Look at Paul's description of the war we are waging in 2 Corinthians 10:3-5. What is the key mentioned at the end of verse 5?

We have to take captive every thought and undergo a transformation. As we saw with the parable in Matthew 12, we cannot be satisfied with recognizing and removing the lie. We must also work diligently to replace it with truth.

John 8:32 "Then you will know the _____, and the truth will set you _____."

John 17:17 "Sanctify them by _____ _____. Your _____ is _____."

 When we replace a lie with truth, describe what happens.

 What is God's goal, as expressed in 1 Timothy 2:1-7?

 How does 2 Timothy 2:22-26 say that we can obtain the knowledge of the truth?

What does repentance mean? What does it look like?

Repentance—the Total Transformation

How do the following verses describe repentance?

Ephesians 4:20-24

Romans 6:1-7

1 John 1:5-10

In order for there to be transformation of a life lived under lies to a life freed by truth, there must be a death to the former way of life. Let's look at some scriptural contrasts between a life bound by lies and a life that embraces truth.

Describe the contrasts seen in the verses below.

2 Corinthians 4:1-2

Romans 1:18-32

The verses in Romans 1 are quite harsh. It is evident that God does not like when we suppress the truth or exchange the truth for a lie (v. 18 & 25).

 Does this make Him an angry God or a jealous God? What's the difference?

 Remember God's goal as expressed in 1 Timothy 2:1-7? How does a life burdened by lies hinder us from that goal?

Even as I worked on the writing of these chapters, Satan was attacking me with lies I have held onto in the past. I include here a portion of a prayer I wrote during that time:

Father, I do long to be free of the shackles of these lies. The cold nature of these chains is a reminder of my humanity and of what I wished were better or different times. But I have to trust that You have a better future for me—that You long to free me and make me whole in You.

If I cannot trust that, trust You, then I remain in the hopeless bondage of lies. Faith hope, and love. But the greatest of these is love. I long to put my faith in You as You fill me with hope, a product of Your love. Give me the strength to cling to truth, to hope—to reclaim the abundant life that can only be attained through You and through a rejection of the lies and their control over me.

I wish I could avoid the pain of learning. I wish I could teach in theory and not in so much practice and personal example. I wish this weren't a part of You answering my prayer, "Here am I. Send me!" but I thank You that the pain is not in vain and that You can receive the glory for healing and teaching that come from it.

The biggest truths that I know I need to cling to are that You love me, and that You want what's best for me. If I can trust You and trust that, the rest falls into place and all other truths in Scripture are honored.

I feel a literal burden lifted from my chest by verbalizing this burden of lies to You. So, why do I avoid going through this process and coming to You with it?

Please forgive me. I approach this writing with a greater spirit of humility and reverence. **I have even avoided going to Your Word, knowing that it will call me to things that I may not want to have to put into practice.**

I've faced so much change in the past year that I'm unsure of what I can even plan toward or count on anymore. I don't want to have to make any more changes or learn any more lessons, so I avoid going to Your Word and being cut again by its truth. By doing that, I am allowing Satan to make a foothold a stronghold and continue to entrap me with his lies.

Is the spirit of my prayer familiar to you? Take a moment to express to God your own frustration with lies or strongholds in your life, asking Him to lead you to truth. (If there is not enough space below, feel free to write your prayer in a separate notebook or in the Notes pages at the back of the book, pg. 257.)

Hindrances to Truth

 Name five things that you think hinder us from embracing the truth. Circle the one you most struggle with.

Exercise: Since a hindrance can also be seen as a lie, we are going to attack each of the hindrances you listed in the previous question, with the truth of faith, hope, and love.

- ➤ Write the hindrances out on the next page in the *Recognize* column of the Lie/Truth Chart.
- ➤ Then, select which aspect of truth (faith, hope, or love) best dispels the lie for each hindrance in the *Replace* column.
- ➤ Find and write out a verse that dispels the lie and affirms the truth in the *Remember* column. (You can refer back to the verses describing faith, hope, and love in chapter 1 or find your own.)
- ➤ You may add to this Lie/Truth Chart when you meet with your Iron Rose Sisters in the small group setting.

RECOGNIZE the lie (in your own words)	REPLACE the lie with truth (in your own words)	REMEMBER the truth (biblical reference)
Hindrance/Lie #1:	Faith Hope Love	
Hindrance/Lie #2:	Faith Hope Love	
Hindrance/Lie #3:	Faith Hope Love	
Hindrance/Lie #4:	Faith Hope Love	
Hindrance/Lie #5:	Faith Hope Love	

We aren't the only ones that have trouble believing the truth. There was a lie that was "widely circulated among the Jews to this very day" regarding Jesus' body and the resurrection (Matt. 28:11-15).

Why do you think that widely circulated lie was easier to believe than the truth?

The truth of the resurrection requires a change. By declaring the resurrection a lie, the soldiers, the chief priests, and the people in Jesus' time gave Satan the last word. Fear, pride, and other hindrances kept them from embracing the truth. Accepting the truth of the resurrection would have required them to do something about it. A truth of that magnitude cannot be ignored. And once we recognize the lie as a lie and replace it with truth, we can no longer live according to that lie. They had a choice. And we have a choice. Who has the last word in your life?

Truth is Powerful. But Truth Requires a Change

The good news is that if I believe in the truth of the resurrection, I also have the hope of the resurrection in my own life! A new life in Christ (Rom. 6:4-5), with mercies that are new every morning (Lam. 3:22-24), is another promise I can cling to.

There was once a young couple. She was shy and reserved. He was sullen and withdrawn. She had grown up in a church environment. He didn't want anything to do with God or the church.

They were living together and occasionally made an appearance at a church event, but never darkened the doors of the church building. And that is how I came to meet them.

When they came, she knew a few friends and would talk with them while he sat on the couch, ignoring others, wearing all black, almost daring others to approach him.

Their lives had been flooded by Satan's lies about their self-worth, about the church, about Christians, and about God's love. Over time, they noticed the genuine and sincere loving-kindness of other Christians and each began to soften their protective shells.

I began to find opportunity to have more conversations with him and even to study the Bible with her. He was hungry for community and she was hungry for the truth. She craved the life spoken of by the source of living water in the Word (John 4:14).

After much study and a hesitation to "surrender," she was baptized in a frigid outdoor pool in Louisiana at the beginning of January. My fingers numb at the memory of that cold night, but my heart warms, as I don't even have to close my eyes to remember the beaming smile on her face and the joy we shared. She had replaced the lies with truth and was claiming the abundant life from that day forward.

Repentance was no easy road, which is why "surrender" had become our key word in stepping forward on faith in God's power to transform a life. But God honored her commitment to Him and over the course of the next year, the couple was married, he was also baptized, and today they are a blessed, God-fearing family of five that you would not recognize had you met them the first day I had.

They were transformed by truth and the power of the Word, but it was a transformational process that took several years of recognizing the lies and replacing them with truth. As they remembered the truth, their faith strengthened. As they continued to surrender to God's plan, He filled them with hope for a better life. And the love they had for God and one another grew exponentially when authored by God and guided by truth.

They had not only learned the truth, but they proceeded in faith, hope, and love as they put it into practice. What a testimony to God's power to transform and the power of truth in our lives!

A Foundation of Truth, Put into Practice

In full knowledge that I will likely get the children's song stuck in your heads, turn with me to Matthew 7:24-27. This is not just a children's story. It is a powerful teaching of Jesus with an application to truth and lies.

How does Matthew 7:24-27 apply to lies and truth?

I can know the truth, but if I don't put it into practice, what good does it do me (James 1:22-25)?

I will close with this quote of encouragement as we give God the last word of truth and put that truth into practice—a key reflection on how to replace the lie with truth.

It is not the number of books you read, nor the variety of sermons you hear, nor the amount of religious conversation in which you mix, but it is the frequency and earnestness with which you meditate on these things until the truth in them becomes your own and part of your be-ing, that ensures your growth. – F.W. Robertson

As you consider the Common Threads this week, the following two questions may provide additional reflection or inspiration: What is a truth that I know but hesitate to put into practice? What would it look like if I lived by that truth?

Common Threads

An area in which you'd like to grow or bloom—abounding in faith, hope, and love through truth.

_____

_____

A thorn (lie) you'd like to remove and replace with truth.

_____

_____

An area in which you'd like to dig deeper or need someone to hold you accountable (help to recognize the lie or remember the truth).

_____

_____

A verse or truth to remember that speaks to a lie mentioned in this chapter.

_____

_____

CHAPTER 5

Remember the Truth

Truth: The first casualty in time of war. – Boake Carter

When anger blinds the eye, truth disappears. – Famous Proverb

I grew up watching Sesame Street[3]. Big Bird, Cookie Monster, Oscar the Grouch, Grover, and other characters helped shape my childhood through their simple teaching and catchy tunes. As a family, we still sing some of the songs and quote some of the bits from certain episodes.

In one episode, a girl is sent to the store by her mother to pick up a few items. The mom repeats the items several times and works to help the girl remember the short list. The mom works with her so that upon entering the store and being distracted by all of the other merchandise, the girl will remember to come home with "a loaf of bread, a container of milk, and a stick of butter."

At the end of the segment, after struggling to remember the list of items, the girl says with great joy in her voice, "I remember, I remember! A loaf of bread, a container of milk, and a stick of butter."

---

[3] Children's Television Network

To this day, when any of us in the family finally remembers something we have forgotten to tell the others, or asks someone to pick up something at the store, we quote with great joy and a smirk, "I remember, I remember! A loaf of bread, a container of milk, and a stick of butter."

The joy and the smirk come because we can all joke and smile about how forgetful we are. But there is also a sense of longing for a simpler time when all we had to remember was a short list of three items to pick up at the store. There is so much more crammed into our brains that it is easy to lose sight of the spiritually important things to remember.

Remember to Give God the Last Word

We are forgetful by nature. **God knows how forgetful we are and throughout the centuries has provided us with reminders of His faithfulness, His sovereignty, and His love.**

In reference to the Lie/Truth Chart, the *Remember* column is a specific scripture that speaks to the truth, giving God the last word. For that very reason, in this chapter, "Remember the Truth," we will focus on submerging ourselves in the Word, the best way to remember the truth.

Even as we look at a plethora of verses in this chapter, remembering the power of the truth in God's Word, may we not forget: Truth is powerful because God is truth. Jesus Himself said, "I am the way, the truth and the life. No one comes to the father, except through me" (John 14:6).

And as we strive to remember the truth from God's Word and give Him the last word, I invite you to remember this simple truth: "Faith, hope, and love. But the greatest of these is love" (1 Cor. 13:13). God is love and His love is perfect (1 John 4:7-19).

God Remembers

Even God takes the time to remember His covenant and His promises. What does God remember in each of the following verses?

Genesis 9:15-16

Exodus 2:24

What does God encourage us to remember in Exodus 20:2 before He gives the Israelites the Ten Commandments?

After the Deuteronomy 5 retelling of the Ten Commandments from Exodus 20, Moses summarizes the heart behind God's commands in Deuteronomy 6:1-12.

Based on what we see in Deuteronomy 6, list some of the suggestions for how to keep the most important thing present in our minds, eyes, and hearts. Share three concrete examples of a modern application of these practices.

What is the significance of Deuteronomy 6:12?

Which of the following tools are you most likely to use to help you recall something?

➤ Write it down (on a notecard, a calendar, or Post-It)

➤ Ask someone else to remind you

➤ Set a reminder in your phone

➤ Send yourself an email

➤ Another idea

Positive and Negative Memories

We are most likely to remember something with which we have made an emotional connection. How well do you remember your first crush? Or the tantalizing smell of cookies fresh-baked by grandma? The words to your favorite song?

However, the opposite is also true. The pain associated with a lie can overshadow all other truths and cause our memories to fade.

If we believe a lie long enough, we rewrite history to match our distorted memory. "God has never taken care of me." "God doesn't love me." "I never do what God asks me to do—I never get anything right."

Lies with absolutes "never" or "always" should be red flags. However, God's promises with absolutes are markers on which we can depend.

When we are down or discouraged, all we remember is the negative, not the positive or the promises. We will discuss this further in Chapter 9: Lies We Believe When We're Discouraged.

God Remembers You

The fact that God remembers you was true for Walter, a college student with whom I was working at Louisiana State University (LSU). Walter was feeling especially discouraged and forgotten by God.

While serving as women's campus minister, I would often go to campus to meet with a student and would then walk back through the Student Union and the most people-filled places on campus to see who else I might run into.

On one such day, I planned to meet one student on campus and later ran into no less than eight students or former students of the LSU Christian Student Center (CSC). It was always a joy to "happen" to run into people and catch up, say hello, share an encouraging word, or hear what was going on in their lives. A simple smile from a Christian sister and friend often served as a reminder that God, too, was smiling down on them.

On that particular afternoon, I was also delivering copies of the *40 days with Jesus, 40 days of Prayer* booklet that our students had helped write. I had one copy left and was finally headed back to the CSC to hop in my car and make a later appointment with someone.

Walking out of the Student Union, I paused to reply to a text and, while I'm fairly good at texting and walking, I felt like the Spirit kept urging me to stop, send the text, and then continue on my way. I finally stepped to the side of the sidewalk, at the end of a stone handrail, and finished my text. As I hit send, I looked up and just a few steps ahead of me was one of our students, Walter. I called out his name and he turned, confirming his earlier suspicion that it was I standing there. He said the Atlanta Braves shirt I was wearing was his biggest clue.

He never walked through that part of campus, especially not at that time of day, and was shocked to have run into me. We talked for a while about his day, his week, his frustrations… and I was able to encourage him about some challenging life situations he was facing. Before we said goodbye, I was able to give him the final copy of the *40 days with Jesus, 40 days of Prayer* booklet, which he had been unable to pick up yet—a providential encounter, for sure.

We both continued on our way uplifted and encouraged, knowing that God had provided a divine appointment, not a chance meeting. Walter was reminded of the truth that he is loved by God and not forgotten. God got the last word in Walter's life that day, not Satan's discouraging thoughts and lies.

It can be hard, at times, to discern the Spirit's leading, but sometimes it's as simple as following the urge to pause on the sidewalk and send a text before hurrying on so that God can use you to bless someone's life—to let them know that they are important enough to God that He would send someone along their path with an encouraging word, the good news of the gospel (like Philip in Acts 8), or a simple smile and a hug.

May we be open to divine appointments God may place along our path and may we share the God stories, giving Him the glory for the way He works even in the smallest details of our lives.

God Stories Refresh Our Memory

Those "God stories,' as I call them, are one of the ways in which I am better able to remember the truth of God's promises and provision. They are stories from everyday life that testify to the living and active hand of God. These stories renew my faith, fill me with hope, and remind me of God's love when I feel far from it.

And I need these stories to refresh my memory and give God the last word. My memory is not what it used to be. People have often said that I have a great memory, but it is only because I write things down. When we write something down, we create a more permanent record that we can use to refresh our memories when they fade—when we feel our faith growing weak, our hope disappearing, or God's love for us non-existent.

Scripture serves as a book full of God stories.

Take some time to write out at least one of your God stories. Be prepared to share it with others as an invitation to the abundant life—to see God's hand working in their lives as well and a reminder that God has the last word. (Feel free to use the Notes section at the back of the book, pg. 257.)

God Established Reminders for His People

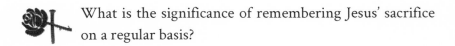 God has always set up ways for us to remember. What practice did He establish for the Israelites to remember how He rescued them from slavery in Egypt? See Deuteronomy 16:1, Exodus 12:24-28. (For the full story, read all of Ex. 12.)

What was the reminder of redemption established in the book of Esther 9:23-28?

Moving to the New Testament, what is the reminder that Jesus, Himself, established that we should do in remembrance of Him and His sacrifice (1 Cor. 11:23-26; Matt. 26:26-30)?

What is the significance of remembering Jesus' sacrifice on a regular basis?

I have lived in many places and visited churches across the world. One of the most beautiful things is that on a Sunday morning, no matter where I have worshipped, no matter whether or not I understood the language, there was a shared understanding when we ate the bread and drank the cup together.

The Lord's Supper is one of my mom's favorite parts of worship because she can close her eyes and picture each of the other members of the family taking it, in whatever city or country we find ourselves that day.

It is a time that is set aside to reflect and remember. More than 70 times in the Bible, God calls us to "remember." He knows that we are forgetful and that even if we know something, we need to be reminded of it. Peter says in 2 Peter 1:12-13 that He will not cease to remind us of the things we already know, because we are forgetful.

The Joy of Remembering

There is a joy that comes with remembering God's promises, just as there are some things that we never tire of hearing, even if we already knew them at one point. How many times do you want to be reminded that someone loves you? And isn't it nice to be reminded in different ways?

 Name three different ways in which God has personally reminded you of His love or the ways in which you have seen Him do so for others.

As we take the time to remember God's love, we are filled by His truth about us, not the lies with which Satan bombards us, thus giving God the last word. The book of John mentions some form of the word truth (truth, true, or truly) 55 times. He not only talks about what truth is, but how we can come to know it and be reminded of it. John has quickly become one of my favorite books of the Bible because of his frequent references to love and truth. Let's look at some of the verses in John that describe truth.

 What is the significance of Christ as the embodiment of truth (John 1:14, 17, and 14:6)?

What have we been promised in John 14:16-17, 15:26-27, and 16:13?

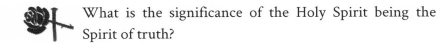 What is the significance of the Holy Spirit being the Spirit of truth?

God speaks truth; Christ embodies truth; the Spirit reminds us of truth. It's a three-fold promise. What is the significance of that promise in our daily lives? Explain how that truth-filled promise strengthens faith, gives hope, and demonstrates love.

Remembering the truth allows God to have the last word—not our fears, not the lies, not the pain, nor the despair. The truth of God's Word cuts through lies like nothing else. The Bible describes the Word as a cutting sword on two occasions:

Ephesians 6:17 and Hebrews 4:12. And it is a blade that never dulls.

The Spiritual Battle of Lies and Truth

Let's look at the entire section in Ephesians 6, verses 10-18. What is Paul talking about?

 How does acknowledging the fight against the lies of Satan as a spiritual battle help us as we wage war with him and strive to remember the truth?

 Why do you think Paul compared truth with a belt?

Which is the only offensive piece of armor—one not designed to defend, but to attack?

 Describe three ways in which the Word is a weapon of attack in the spiritual battle of lies and truth.

According to Hebrews 4:12, how is the sword of the Word of God described? What is it able to cut through?

 Do we trust God's Word to cut through the lies and give the final word? Why or why not?

What happens when the truth hurts and we prefer to stay with the familiar lie, setting aside the stinging truth?

Yes, when truth cuts, it wounds, but it is a pain of healing, like when a burn patient's old skin is scrubbed, in order to allow the new skin to grow.

One of the most vital keys to remember is one that applies to God's Word spoken into our lives and to our words of truth spoken into the lives of others. How do we see that truth expressed in 1 Corinthians 13:1-3 and Ephesians 4:15?

Why does *that* truth make a difference in how we handle *all* truth?

Do you truly believe that God has spoken the things in His Word out of love?

How do we process His truths differently when seen through the lens of love?

God speaks truth into our lives as an outpouring of His immeasurable love for us. But, for many, it can be hard to trust that depth of true love. And for others, it has not been an immediate belief—rather one they have come to over time and with practice. You can come to own that truth as well—to hear all God's truths with His loving voice.

The truth becomes easier to recognize the more you know the speaker—"There's no way he could've said that because I know him." The more we come to know God and dwell in His Word, the easier it is to recognize the lie, hear the love in His voice, and trust the truth of His promises.

Just as we saw in the example of Eve, Satan wants us to believe that God's truths are there to cause us pain, to miss out on fun, to hinder us from living the life we want to live. But God, as our Creator, knows what is best for us, and longs for us to have an abundant and blessed life in Him.

As we continue through the chapters that highlight personal lies in our lives, let us all **remember the ultimate truth that God is love (1 John 4:7-8), and that all of the truths He will remind us of through His Word are spoken out of love and a deep desire to bless us as His children.**

The pain of truth or the sting of lies can cause us to lose sight of God's love. We believe the lies rather than trust the ultimate truth-teller. Lies rob us of hope and fill us with fear. But **truth is powerful and redeeming—able to cut through the lies and replace fear with faith, doubt with hope, and despair with love.**

"May the God of hope fill you with all joy and peace as you trust in him, so that you may overflow with hope by the power of the Holy Spirit" (Rom. 15:13).

One more God story to close this chapter:

Giving Faith in God the Last Word

My chest was tight and my head was swimming as I totaled up how much I had personally invested in Iron Rose Sister Ministries (IRSM) in the ministry's first six months. The weightiest and final straw came after authorizing the advance purchase of 2,000 copies of the 1st small group Bible study book, *Human AND Holy*, and 3,000 copies of the Spanish version, *Humano Y Santo*.

My inadequacies were rearing their ugly heads, as I doubted the wisdom of making this decision. I had not come to this recent resolution on my own, but made it in counsel with the Board of Directors for IRSM. We all agreed that it was a great savings in an effort to reduce the overhead cost for each of the books, especially as they are subsidized and distributed to Latin America, and to many women and churches that are in need of such materials and encouragement.

But as a very large chunk of my savings went to the advance purchase of the books, my trust in God and His plan for the ministry wavered. I started counting my blessings and continued praying, but the tightness in my chest would not go away...

I got a few more things done that afternoon in an effort to distract myself and headed to church a short time later. That Wednesday evening, we continued our discussion in the book of Matthew and "happened" to be in chapter 14, which includes the story of Jesus feeding the 5,000 with the five loaves and two fish. Someone mentioned the disciples' lack of faith and made a comment about how many miracles the disciples had seen and yet they still doubted.

Well, I get it. I am definitely one of those disciples, a follower of Jesus that has seen so many miracles in the past, one that has been blessed countless times with God's provision, but still doubts. Oh ye of little faith. Yep. That's me. "Little faith," party of one. Party of many. Because I know you've been there too.

As I was reminded that night, **time in the Word and with other Christians gave God the last word, and not my fears or insecurities**. The last word was one of faith in the One who provides.

May we all be reminded of the overabundant examples of God's provision, from the stories in our own lives to the multiplying of the five loaves and two fish with twelve basketfuls left over! I thank God for graciously reminding me of that one Wednesday night. My fears are still very real and very present as I continue to move forward with IRSM, but I have been able to go back to the five loaves and two fish as a reminder of God's provision and blessing.

Remember: Recognize the lies and replace them with truth. **Remember:** God's Word has the power to cut through the lies and remind us of truth. **Remember:** Always give God the last word of faith, hope, and love.

Common Threads

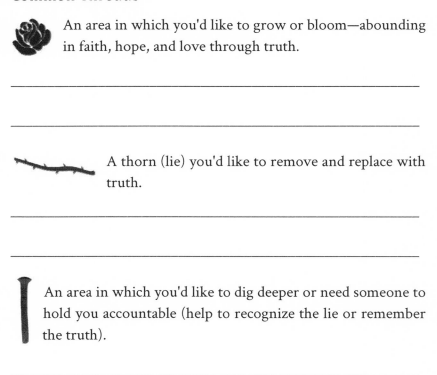

An area in which you'd like to grow or bloom—abounding in faith, hope, and love through truth.

_____

_____

A thorn (lie) you'd like to remove and replace with truth.

_____

_____

An area in which you'd like to dig deeper or need someone to hold you accountable (help to recognize the lie or remember the truth).

_____

_____

A verse or truth to remember that speaks to a lie mentioned in this chapter.

_____

_____

CHAPTER 6

Lie: I Am Alone

The eye sees only what the mind is prepared to comprehend. – Robertson Davies (Canadian author and playwright)

The whole conviction of my life now rests upon the belief that loneliness, far from being a rare and curious phenomenon, peculiar to myself and to a few other solitary men, is the central and inevitable fact of human existence. – Thomas Wolfe

Silence and solitude can be great facilitators of time alone with God and a deepening of spiritual disciplines. However, they are also some of the greatest tools of the enemy.

Quiet moments with the heavenly Father are a precious commodity, but too much time alone with my thoughts allows lies to resurface, insecurities to take hold, and doubts to arise.

When Satan gets me alone, I feel isolated, abandoned, and come to believe that no one understands me. I feel alone in my pain and that I have no one to support me. It's from there I can quickly slip into preferring to be alone. It's not hard to choose this. It's easier than being rejected or feeling like the victim of other people's choices. Rejection and loneliness are familiar feelings, so why fight them?

When God gets me alone, I am warmed by His embrace, reminded of His love, filled with His presence, and surrounded by His mercy. I know I am not alone in my pain and that He has given me the church as a source of support. I can choose to spend time alone or with others because I am at peace in my relationship with my Father. Feelings of rejection and loneliness can raise their ugly heads, but they become occasions to run back to my Father for affirmation and peace.

Don't Go It Alone

As we begin with this chapter to more directly fight Satan's lies, do not attempt to do so alone. You will be equipped with tools to recognize a lie, replace the lie with truth, and remember the truth when attacked by Satan, but it is not a battle to be fought alone. While a lion seeks to isolate its prey so it can more easily attack, **Satan's goal is to get us alone and make us weak for his attacks.** One of the primary goals of Iron Rose Sister Ministries and the motivation behind preparing this Bible study to be used in the context of a small group is so that Satan cannot accomplish that goal.

Your Iron Rose Sisters are among those who encourage, challenge, and remind you of the truth that you are not alone. Through prayer and the encouragement of Iron Rose Sisters in my life, I would not be where I am today—growing in faith and being transformed through the process of recognizing the lies, replacing them with truth, and remembering the truth.

I can picture some of those sisters sitting with me over the years, speaking truths into my life, and filling my spirit with hope. Please allow me to return the favor—to provide you with the opportunity to join together as Christian women—Iron Rose Sisters—and speak loving truth into each other's lives.

The Power of Faith

Let's start with an exercise to be done in the group: An affirmation that none of us is alone on this journey and that we can **work together to strengthen each other's faith.**

There was a paralyzed man brought to Jesus in an unconventional way in Mark 2. He was lowered on a mat through the roof by four of his friends. It's a powerful story of friendship, support, faith, and yet another opportunity that Jesus took to teach.

Read the entire story in Mark 2:1-12.

 Which character do you most identify with? Why?

Whose faith prompted Jesus to forgive the man's sins (v. 5)?

Yes! It was the friends' faith, not the invalid's faith, which prompted action. **We may feel alone in our struggle and without enough faith to step out of the situation, but that's where those who walk with us in Christ carry us through.** At times, it can be easier to believe in healing for someone else than it can be to believe it for ourselves. So, let's lower each other through the roof and lift each other up to the Father! We are not alone, and we do not have to rely on our own strength.

Exercise:

(Note: Even if you are currently studying *Who Has the Last Word?* alone, you can still participate in this exercise. If you are completing the book by yourself, I encourage you to go back through it later with a group of Christian sisters who can serve as iron sharpening iron, encouraging and inspiring you to be as beautiful as a rose in spite of a few thorns—Iron Rose Sisters. You also will be able to do the same for them!)

I encourage each of you to take a moment to call on two to four Christians—possibly the other sisters in your small group—to lift you in prayer. This may be a prayer for healing, for strength in the struggle to embrace truth, or for faith to remember that you are not alone. Commit to lifting them up in prayer, as well.

Just as the friends did for the paralyzed man in Mark 2, take turns putting each other on the mat in prayer. Write your name on the bottom of the first mat on the next page, and the names of those who are praying for you on the four handles of the mat. Trust in their faith for healing as they lift you to the Father.

Do the same for the others for whom you are praying. Put their names on the bottom of the other mats and your name, along with the other pray-ers, on the four handles of the remaining mats. Spend some time in prayer over each individual. It is an honor to bring these requests before our loving Heavenly Father who wants to heal us, free us from lies, and remind us that we are not alone.

"And the prayer offered in faith will make the sick person well; the Lord will raise them up. If they have sinned, they will be forgiven" (James 5:16).

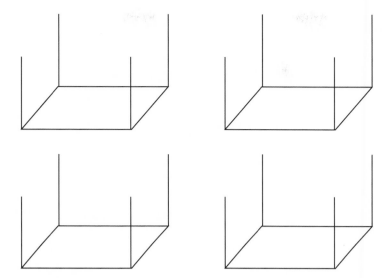

You are not alone! When Satan succeeds in isolating us, one of the first lies we believe is that we are alone in that struggle. Even though Solomon tells us that "there is nothing new under the sun," (Eccl. 1:9), Satan clouds our memory and judgment when it comes to remembering that we are not alone or the only one facing that struggle.

Let me share a story that explains this.

Two Sisters, One Lie

One night, in a small-group Bible study, I shared a lesson with Hispanic sisters at a church in Houston. The class was about truth and lies, and contained some of the same material from this book.

The class was well received and at the end, I asked each of the ladies to partner with the woman next to her and share a lie of Satan she personally battles. They were also instructed to find a verse in the Bible that spoke a truth to cut through that lie, just like we're doing in this book. It was beautiful to see them sharing and flipping through their Bibles.

As they were finishing up, two women excitedly asked me to come over and talk with them. They just had to share with me that they battle the exact same lie: that they don't have time to read their Bibles! They were able to encourage each other mutually in the truth and promises of Scripture. Phone numbers were exchanged so that they could continue to encourage each other during the week. Before I walked away, they read me the verse that gave them so much hope and joy—**the truth that cut through Satan's lie and gave God the last word in their lives:**

> *Be strong and very courageous. Be careful to obey all the law my servant Moses gave you; do not turn from it to the right or to the left, that you may be successful wherever you go. Keep this Book of the Law always on your lips; meditate on it day and night, so that you may be careful to do everything written in it. Then you will be prosperous and successful.* (Josh. 1:7-8)

God gave Joshua a beautiful reminder for the third time in that chapter, "Be strong and very courageous." May God continue to bless each of us with encouraging reminders, as He did for those two ladies that evening. And may He continue to use Iron Rose Sister Ministries to equip, inspire, and empower women in their relationship with God and others.

The Lie that I Am Alone

 What is a struggle in which you feel alone?

Name a character in the Bible that shared a similar struggle or offered encouragement in the struggle you face.

"Rejoice with those who rejoice. Mourn with those who mourn" (Rom. 12:15). We long to share in community during the tough times, but also during the times of blessing!

 List three blessings from the past week with which you can rejoice with your Iron Rose Sisters.

Describe the promises in each of the following verses as they negate the lie "I am alone."

John 14:16-21

1 John 4:7-18

Matthew 28:16-20

1 Corinthians 12:12-27

Which promise most resonates with you? Why?

You are Loved. You are Prayed for. And You are Not Alone.

As evidenced in these verses and reflected through the exercise inspired by Mark 2, I want you to fully comprehend these three things: You are loved. You are prayed for. And you are not alone.

Did you hear that? **You are loved. You are prayed for. And you are not alone.** I'm not referring to sister-so-and-so who you think *deserves* the love and the prayers. I'm talking about you!

One of the designs of studying these lessons and combatting these lies in the context of a small group is so that we have the opportunity to affirm that we are not alone in our struggles. There are other women with whom we can pray and be encouraged. You can be Iron Rose Sisters together—Christian sisters that have committed to praying for you, encouraging you, and reminding you of truth when Satan's whispered lies turn to shouts in our heads.

When we feel alone, all other lies are compounded. Even now, as we strive to dispel the lie that you are alone, Satan may be bombarding you with lies and discrediting these truths spoken over you. Don't give him the last word!

And while you may still have times when you feel alone, may you be comforted by the truths in this chapter to know that you are never alone.

Lacey's Story

Lacey needed to be reminded that she was not alone. Shortly after her sixteenth birthday, in a whirlwind of doctor's appointments, x-rays, whispered conversations, concerned looks, and consultations, Lacey was sent to St. Jude's Children's Hospital in Memphis, Tennessee. An osteosarcoma tumor had broken through the bone in her left leg about an inch and a half under her kneecap.

Lacey and her mom were not close before, but when she was yanked out of her junior year of high school so she could move out of state to fight the aggressive cancer, she developed a new appreciation and respect for her mom. Lacey's mom gave encouragement and a never-ending supply of Yoo-hoo Chocolate Drink™ through chemo and multiple surgeries, including the removal of the left leg bone and calf muscle.

Lacey's mom was a rock for her daughter, but Lacey still felt very alone. Before leaving for Memphis, she felt as though she wasn't the most popular teenager in the youth group, and was unsure how many people in her home church in Baton Rouge even knew her. Now, she was three states away and all alone.

But as she was bombarded with texts, cards, calls, and notes that told her how much she was loved, that she was prayed for, and that she was not alone, the message began to sink in. To this day, an encouragement pillow signed by dozens of members of the church is a treasured possession as it reminds Lacey of the constant prayers and support of her church family.

When I asked Lacey if I could share her story and the way that God and the church helped her battle the lie that she was alone, she responded, "I would ABSOLUTELY LOVE FOR YOU TO

USE MY STORY! I believe that I went through all that I did for a reason, and that reason is to help others who feel hopeless or who are going through what I went through. I'm proof that cancer is survivable, and if I didn't share my story to help others, even though it's really hard sometimes, everything I went through would have been for nothing!"

She continued, "James 5:11 is my favorite verse because Job is my favorite story in the Bible. Satan tried to tell me that because I was going through a hard time far away from home that I wasn't going to make it because I was alone. **But God showed me that I had a church family that stood behind me more than I ever thought they would because I mattered more to God than I thought I did.** Amen! I applaud Lacey for sharing her story and for giving God the last word.

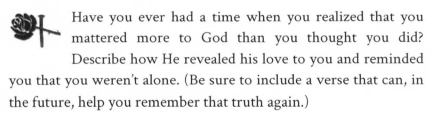

Have you ever had a time when you realized that you mattered more to God than you thought you did?

Describe how He revealed his love to you and reminded you that you weren't alone. (Be sure to include a verse that can, in the future, help you remember that truth again.)

Not Alone in Church

God has given us the blessing of the church to join together in times of rejoicing and in times of trouble—to be a body and a family. You may feel like the only broken one, but Jesus affirms that it is not the healthy who need a doctor, but the sick (Mark 2:17).

You may not have the best model of family support in your own life, but God has provided us with the opportunity to begin anew with our church family. If your wounds come from your church family, I want to encourage you with the truth that your past experiences do not mean that you are destined or condemned to be alone. We will explore that concept more in chapter 10, Lie: God is Punishing Me for My Past.

With more than fifty verses throughout the New Testament that describe the "one another" relationships in the church, there is great merit in taking a deeper look at the church and her relationships. We will discuss more about the church in chapter 8, Lie: I Have to Do It on My Own.

But in the context of this lie, "I am alone," we must remember that we cannot come to know the blessing of the body if we are not connected or in relationship with it. My encouragement to you is that you allow this interactive Bible study with your Iron Rose Sisters to be a brand new experience—no matter what your history with your family or with the church.

God is our greatest comfort, and when we feel let down and alone, we can remember that His "love never fails, never gives up, never runs out on me."[4] God's love and commitment to us measures above and beyond all the love the world offers. Let's give His true love the last word.

The truth is that, like Lacey, like the two sisters who struggled with the same lie, we are not alone. **We can remember the truth that we are each the beloved daughter of a heavenly Father**

---

[4] Chris McClarney, original artist

who longs to bless us with community, fellowship, and relationship that can be found only in Him.

The Unmet Expectations of Relationship

As a single girl, those truths are hard to remember when I am bombarded by the world's view of what it means to not be alone: Fall in love, marry, have 2.5 kids, a white picket fence, and a recipe-swapping relationship with your in-laws. Can you relate to this disconnect? Or what about to the advertising images that not being alone mean you're surrounded by friends who are constantly going out and doing things? Or even to the religious message that being married means you will never feel alone?

I believe that Genesis 2:18, "It is not good for the man to be alone," does not refer exclusively to marriage. We are designed to be in relationship. **And when it comes to the lie of being alone, Satan camps out on the unmet expectations of relationship.**

Which of the following three lies do you most recognize as an attack of Satan in your life?

➤ Being single or single-again means always being alone.

➤ Being married means never feeling alone.

➤ Being married means always being alone.

All three are lies! **If we do not find our fulfillment in God, we will** *always* **feel alone no matter what our marital status or relationship dynamic.** Personally, this is one of the ways in which Satan attacks me with an intense vengeance. And I avoid those thoughts even more when I am alone because they affirm the lies that I am unlovable, rejected, and destined always to be alone.

My head knows this is not true, but my heart often aches to be loved in the ways that many know love, through a Christian partnership in marriage. I know it is not the solution to loneliness, nor will it fulfill all my longings or desires, but to have begun to taste it and then have it taken away makes it all the more tempting. (I suffered a broken engagement in 2012.)

Satan's lies come flooding in, causing me to not want to be alone with those thoughts or to ask God the deeper questions that come with them. Sometimes, I don't know that I want to hear the answer to my prayers if it is that I should stay single for the rest of my life, married to Christ and His ministry. Other days, it is exactly what I want to hear.

Fear keeps me from the truth and overshadows my faith.

 What truth do you fear?

 What lie do you allow to overshadow your faith?

Even as I worked on the chapters of this book, I was plagued by dreams, maybe even nightmares, and restless sleep, as I wrestled to cling to truth. Satan was fighting to have me hold onto the lie and lose the desired peace only God provides.

I was living in fear, not faith, hindering God from having the last word.

The lie deceptively brought me false comfort because even the rejection of love meant that I had a glimpse of what was not to be. I clung to the memory, but it only tethered me to the past.

Father, I wish I didn't continue to struggle with the same lies, the same thorns in my flesh. They are my constant reminder of my need for You, which is one of the reasons I fear that You will never provide me with a partner with whom I can walk through life.

Even as I moved toward marriage and looked to a man to provide for me and our future children, I feared how that could happen on one salary. Now, in a twist of irony, I have no salary and am looking to You and Your provision for all things.

These lessons have been difficult to accept, and I despise the pain with which they have been learned. I wish there was a different way, but when I go back to embracing the lies, the cut of truth stings again.

Even as some of you read my feelings of frustration and loneliness, I know you long to speak truth and encouragement into my life, to remind me of God's faithfulness, and to challenge me to keep moving forward in faith as I allow God to use me. For that, I thank you.

I have not made it through the process of battling those lies on my own. I have been blessed by the invaluable support of those around me. They have held up the banner of truth when I feel beaten down by the lies.

Their support has been one of the biggest testimonies to the truth that I am not alone—not in relationship, nor in my struggle with this and other lies. With their help, I was able to recognize the lie that I am alone. I replaced that lie with the truth that I have a loving Father who has promised to never leave me nor forsake me (Josh. 1:5). I am also surrounded by a loving family and church family that lift me up in prayer and encourage me with reminders of that truth.

I have put my own transformation from lie to truth in the Lie/Truth Chart on the next page. And I ask you to **select at least three lies to replace with truth**, then find a truth in Scripture to remember it by.

1. Ask yourself, "What lie about being alone do I most identify with?"

2. **Pick three** or put a different lie in your own words in the blank portions of the chart below.

3. For the three lies you selected, fill in the rest of the chart *Replace the Lie with Truth* (in your own words) and *Remember the Truth* (biblical reference).

4. If you get stumped about verses with truths to remember, feel free to refer back to verses mentioned in this chapter or earlier chapters.

Specifically regarding the promise that we are not alone, here are a few more verses of promise: Psalm 23, Isaiah 41:10 & 13, Mathew 1:22-23.

RECOGNIZE the lie (in your own words)	REPLACE the lie with truth (in your own words)	REMEMBER the truth (biblical reference)
I will always be alone because I will never be married.	Marriage is not the only way to define relationship. God has promised to never leave me nor forsake me, and has blessed me with a loving and supportive Christian family that stands by my side.	"I will never leave you nor forsake you." **Josh. 1:5** "A cord of three strands is not quickly broken." **Eccl. 4:12**
I am alone in my pain.		
I have the support of no one.		
God has abandoned me.		
I want to be alone. I have chosen this. It's easier than being rejected.		
I don't need anyone. I do best by myself.		
I'm the only one that struggles with _____ sin.		

RECOGNIZE	REPLACE	REMEMBER
No one understands me.		
I am the only one trying to do what is right.		
I am the only Christian in my class, job, family, etc.		

Spend some time on your own, in communion with the Father, allowing Him to remind you of the promises found in the truth of the Word. **Give God the last word in your life, especially as we recognize and replace the lie, "I am alone."**

When you gather with your Iron Rose Sisters, take the opportunity to share the different ways in which Satan attacks, realizing that even if the specific attacks in our personal lives are different for everyone, we are fighting the same enemy, and that God is on our side! Spend some time in prayer over the Lie/Truth Chart, reminding each other of the truth. **Prayer is vital in our spiritual battle and is a reminder of the presence of God with us.**

Common Threads

An area in which you'd like to grow or bloom—abounding in faith, hope, and love through truth.

_____

_____

A thorn (lie) you'd like to remove and replace with truth.

_____

_____

An area in which you'd like to dig deeper or need someone to hold you accountable (help to recognize the lie or remember the truth).

_____

_____

A verse or truth to remember that speaks to a lie mentioned in this chapter.

_____

_____

CHAPTER 7

Lie: Happiness is the Ultimate Goal

Feeling better has become more important to us than finding God. – Larry Crabb

In our age, as in every age, people are longing for happiness, not realizing that what they are looking for is holiness. – Jerry L. Walls

I have never met a soul who has set out to satisfy the Lord and has not been satisfied himself. – Watchman Nee

There are three kinds of people: those who have sought God and found him, and these are reasonable and happy; those who seek God and have not yet found him, and these are reasonable and unhappy; and those who neither seek God nor find him, and these are unreasonable and unhappy. – Blaise Pascal

"And they lived happily ever after..." But when does real life ever really end like the fairy tale?

We grow up hearing unrealistic stories of princesses like Snow White, Belle, Jasmine, and Ariel. Our dreams are tainted and our expectations unrealistic as we launch into adulthood searching for our own version of "happily ever after."

We compare the fairytale classics to our own stories, which fall far short of our idealized notions of happiness. Sleeping Beauty is awakened by a delicate kiss from Prince Charming, not a half-hearted peck from an unshaven face with bad breath. Cinderella has a team of beauty consultants that transform her bedhead, spit-up-stained clothes, and worn out tennis shoes into a dazzling up-do with a designer gown and glass slippers; not to mention a fairy godmother that converts her fender-dented minivan into a horse drawn carriage. The beast we married is not being transformed into the handsome price we thought we could change like Belle did.

And who said happily ever after had to include a man anyway? In Disney's *Frozen*[5], (spoiler alert) I was thrilled that the "act of true love" that saves both Anna and Elsa at the end of the movie was not true love's kiss, but rather the sacrificial love of one for another.

"Greater love has no one than this: to lay down one's life for one's friends" (John 15:13).

So, you think God maybe had it right all along? True love and happiness as God designed them do not match Hollywood's distorted version of these ill-defined terms portrayed in movies and TV shows—nor do they compare to the lies Satan promotes through short-term gratification.

Satan has been attempting these schemes since the beginning of time: the pursuit of happiness at the expense of anything else. Today, this can take the form of instant gratification, but we don't have the corner on that social dynamic.

---

[5] Walt Disney Animation Studios, 2013.

Short-term Gratification versus Eternal Blessings

The Israelites grew impatient as Moses went up the mountain to receive the Ten Commandments. They preferred the short-term gratification of the golden calf at the base of Mt. Sinai to the eternal blessings promised by God to those who trust and obey Him.

Israel sought after other gods and other pursuits, but no false idol ever measured up to Jehovah God.

Anything that is not God will not make us truly happy.

What does Zechariah 10:2 say about the nature of idols?

Another name for an idol is a counterfeit god. Timothy Keller defines a counterfeit god as

... anything so central and essential to your life that, should you lose it, your life would feel hardly worth living. An idol has such a controlling position in your heart that you can spend most of your passion and energy, your emotional and financial resources, on it without a second thought.[6]

Idols or counterfeit gods come in all shapes and forms—personal, physical, emotional, intellectual, cultural... They give us a false sense of security and happiness. And they can be anything that we value more than God Himself, even good things—

---

[6] Keller, Timothy. *Counterfeit Gods* (London: Penguin, 2009), xviii.

blessings from God that take the place of Him as our number one priority.

 What do modern-day idols look like? List five common idols and star the one that you most often go to for happiness.

Place that starred false idol in the blank of the first and second columns of the first row of the Lie/Truth Chart below. Then fill in the *Replace* column of the second row with a truth in your own words and a verse to *Remember the Truth* in that same row.

RECOGNIZE the lie (in your own words)	REPLACE the lie with truth (in your own words)	REMEMBER the truth (biblical reference)
1. _____ makes me happy.	_____ may meet a temporary need, but will never fulfill me, as God does.	"And my God will meet all your needs, according to the riches of his glory in Christ Jesus." Phil. 4:19
2. I know what will make me happy… I know what is best for my happiness.		

One truth an Iron Rose Sister friend shared in her *Replace* column was: **The quickest path to happiness is to agree with God.** Do you agree? Why or why not?

When we pursue happiness as our primary goal, we lose sight of the true source of joy, happiness, and fulfillment. **Happiness can be a secondary benefit of a life lived with God, but we are not guaranteed a happy life.**

Seek God and find happiness (Matt. 6:33). Seek happiness and find emptiness.

Happiness and God

What details to we learn about happiness according to each of the following verses?

Ecclesiastes 2:24-26

Matthew 25:21, 23

Psalm 68:3

James 5:13

Does that mean that God is concerned about our happiness?

Let's look at it from a different angle… **If we are called to be transformed into God's image (2 Cor. 3:18), consider what characteristics of the Lord we should emulate—what makes** *Him* **happy or sad.**

Is God happy all the time? Of course not! Let's ponder a few things that make God happy and others that sadden Him.

 List three of the biggest sources of joy for our Heavenly Father. Be sure to include a verse that affirms His pleasure.

 Name three things that make God sad or upset. Don't forget to include the biblical reference here, as well.

Take a moment to reflect on how the weight of sin, disobedience, and other aspects of the ugliness of this world will never, and should never, make us happy. So, is happiness the ultimate goal?

Is God Concerned with My Happiness?

The martyr's lie says, "God didn't want me to be happy anyway."

The egotist's lie says, "God wants me to be happy no matter what/at all cost."

 For you personally, which is the bigger lie that you battle: God wants me to be happy or God doesn't want me to be happy?

 So, is God concerned with my happiness? Or what is it that He is *more* concerned about having the last word on?

Happiness versus Holiness and Obedience

God cares more about our holiness than our happiness.

For example, no child is happy to be punished. A two-year-old tests his boundaries; seeking safety in the world he is learning and exploring.

Read Hebrews 12:4-11. According to verses 10 and 11, what is the fruit of God's discipline? (Hint: It's not our happiness!)

Happiness should never be at the expense of holiness, righteousness, or obedience.

What is one of the ways that God brings about our holiness (sanctification) according to John 17:17?

Read 1 Samuel 15:18-23. What did God desire above all things?

God cares more about our obedience than our happiness.

If we love God, we will obey His commands (John 14:23). And if we obey His commands, we dwell in His love (1 John 3:24). What better way to achieve deep, lasting happiness and security than in communion with God!

Yet, in the same way that our love for others can fade over time, our love for God may also waver. Love is a choice. Obedience is a choice. We may not feel like obeying God, but, no matter what, we are going to either obey sin or God (Rom. 6:16-22). It's our choice. Love God or love sin. Listen to lies or truth. Give God the last word or allow the father of lies to distort the issue.

And, to be honest, sometimes, I just don't feel like it. But then I remember that it is not about how I feel. I can think that "God would want me to be a happy—to obey because I feel like it—from the heart," but that's another alluring lie of Satan. If Satan can get us to think that our feelings matter more than our obedience, we are trapped in a dangerous lie.

Remember: My obedience matters more than my happiness…

Faith-filled Obedience, Feelings will Follow

(Written around the three-year anniversary of a most-unhappy time in my life.)

Always the social butterfly and extrovert, my closet introvert has dominated the past few years. That may not have been obvious to most or evident to those who even know me best.

Before the emotional trauma of my fiancé ending our relationship, I had never experienced social anxiety or panic attacks. Nevertheless, in the months and years following that event, I felt like an unknown extension of myself, or someone who was merely going through the motions of being who I knew I truly was.

It wasn't a mask. I guess you could say that I was trying to fake it until I made it… Because I knew that the truest version of myself was still in there, waiting to reawaken and return to the land of the living.

Severe depression can do that to a person. And it is a process to walk through—notice I didn't say "come out of," because I believe it is a continual journey and struggle for those who face it (which we will explore more in chapter 9: Lies We Believe When We're Discouraged.)

The past three years have been extremely stressful and emotionally intense, for reasons and in ways that are not worth enumerating. **I will not elaborate because my current focus is one of gratefulness.**

Open, honest, and authentic conversation has characterized my interaction with many of you regarding the challenges I have faced. And so, I am thrilled to share with you that over the past few days, I am extremely grateful to have seen my head lift from out of the fog.

Tonight was the first time in a long time that I actually wanted to be a part of church, apart from Sunday morning worship. I sang with abandon, prayed with passion, and greeted others with genuine interest.

Does this mean that what I have been doing for the past three years has been insincere? Was I doing it all for show or just going through the motions? Not at all.

Everything was done on faith. Faith in God to redeem me and restore my first love. Faith in God to continue to guide my steps and clarify my calling. Faith in others to be patient through the process. Faith through the tears, the nightmares, the anxiety, the depression, the pain, the frustrations, the stress...

And now, whether this feeling lasts only for another day or another week, I thank God that, through faith, I reached a point where I truly wanted to go to church tonight—not to fulfill a duty or to do my job, always knowing I would find joy once I got there. Tonight, I finally wanted to go to church to be the church and be with the church, to worship with other Christians—to celebrate our faith by doing and being all of what church is about.

Because faith is not based on a feeling. It is based on obedience and trust in the One who can return us to the truest version of ourselves and transform us more and more into the image of His Son.

So, I invite you to rejoice with me in the power of faith. I encourage you to persevere in faith and hope. And **I pray that God strengthens you to continue to obey through faith,** even if you spend a day, a week, a month, or years "not feeling it."

Joy versus Happiness

Through those challenging and down times, it was very difficult for me to find happiness. But, thankfully, joy and happiness are two different things. The joy of the Lord was my strength in times of weakness (Neh. 8:10).

Happiness is often tied to our circumstances, what "happens." Happiness stems from our own selfish pursuits.

Joy is a God-given blessing—a fruit of the Holy Spirit (Gal. 5:22). We can have joy in trials (James 1:3), and our mourning can be turned to joy (Est. 9:22, Ps. 30:11, 126:5-6, Jer. 31:13).

 Why or in what ways do we get so wrapped up in our longing for happiness instead of trusting God for true joy?

The Pursuit of Happiness

Solomon says that there is nothing new under the sun (Eccl. 1:9). As the recipient of great wisdom and the second wisest man to walk the earth (second only to Jesus), he imparts some of his wisdom regarding the pursuit of happiness in his book, Ecclesiastes.

What does Ecclesiastes 2:10-11 say about the pursuit of pleasure?

Throughout his book of wise musings, Solomon concludes that it is all meaningless. Everything is meaningless—a chasing after the wind. Everything except...

Read Ecclesiastes 12:13-14. How does Solomon instruct us to give God the last word?

Trust and Obey

The chorus of the classic hymn states, "Trust and obey, for there's no other way, to be happy in Jesus, but to trust and obey."

"Your thoughts are not my thoughts, neither are your ways my ways..." (Isa. 55:8-9). We have to trust that our Creator knows how He designed His creation—our inner longings and desires, what fulfills us and brings us true joy. "You will go out in joy and be led forth in peace" (Isa. 55:12).

Because God's wisdom is greater than man's wisdom (James 3:13-18).

But it can be very hard to give God the last word when our happiness is at stake. **Obedience is hardest when we are called to do something that we fear will steal our joy.**

Sarah's Source of Happiness

We longed for a child. I lost count of the prayers I lifted up pleading and begging for a child. Jehovah God had promised to give us more descendants than stars in the sky or sands on the seashore, but as I approached menopause, this seemed more and more impossible.

Women around me had baby after baby and we were still childless. Did God think that I wouldn't be a good mother? What was wrong with me? Wasn't my primary purpose to bear children for my husband? And I couldn't even do that.

Out of love for my husband, I gave him my maidservant so that he might have an heir. What was I thinking? Such a bad idea... Things blew up in my face and not only did she despise me, but acted like she was more of a woman than I was for bearing him a son.

As much as Abraham loved his son, I couldn't bear having them in my house any more. They were sent away and I was still childless. Any distant hope I had of bearing a child was so remote that when some angels visited Abraham and told him that within a year I would bear him a child, I laughed.

Defeated, I had finally made my peace with things. My body had shut down and my expectation of the angel's promise becoming a reality was little to none.

But then it happened—what can only be described as a miracle. I was pregnant! At first, no one believed me. I barely believed it—a woman at my age, with child!

My womb grew and with it, our tremendous love for this promised child—the answer to our prayers and fulfillment of God's covenant.

We named him Isaac, which means laughter. I laughed with overabounding joy every time I spoke his name. "Isaac, you are getting so big!" "Isaac, you can't eat that towel." "Isaac, come wash your hands for dinner..."

The years passed and my newfound happiness was indescribable, unquenchable, and undeniable.

And then the unthinkable happened. God asked Abraham to take our only son, my dear, sweet Isaac, up the mountain and sacrifice him.

Scripture does not clearly state in Genesis 22 whether or not Sarah knew about what God had asked of Abraham, before or after it happened. However, we are going to answer the following questions imagining that God had asked Sarah and not Abraham to sacrifice Isaac.

Based on this story, retold from Genesis 22:1-2 and preceding chapters, how do you think Sarah would react to God calling her to sacrifice her primary source of happiness?

What are your primary sources of happiness? Is it hard to even imagine writing them down right now for fear that God will ask you to sacrifice them?

Through faith, Abraham gave God the last word of truth regarding his ultimate source of happiness.

Look at what Abraham says to his servants before he and Isaac ascend the mountain for the sacrifice in Genesis 22:5. "We will worship and then WE will come back to you" *(emphasis added).*

Abraham is confident that both he and Isaac will return, even after knowing that God has called him to sacrifice his only son, the son he loves.

What is God's response to Abraham in Genesis 22:18? Why does God honor His promise?

Faith and Obedience Lead to Contentment

We are called to step forward in obedience and faith—to give God the last word in all aspects of our lives.

Faith in God's plan, not a watered-down version of it, nor any addition or subtraction from it... **Faith in God's goals**, not my limited perspective of temporary, short-lived, momentary, and fleeting happiness... **Faith in God's timing**, not my expectations of the way I think my life should play out or the way the world describes a "normal" life.

When we are always looking to the "next thing," we rob the present of its joy and its value.

Lie: I'll be happy when I have a boyfriend.

Lie: I'll be happy when I get married.

Lie: I'll be happy when we have kids.

Lie: I'll be happy when the kids are out of diapers.

Lie: I'll be happy when the kids are in school.

Lie: I'll be happy when we get past the teenage years.

Lie: I'll be happy when the kids are out of the house.

Lie: I'll be happy when I get grandkids.

Select one of these lies to place in the Lie/Truth Chart below and write a truth in your own words in the second column.

In the second row, place another lie and truth regarding a current circumstance in your life you wish were different. Then, re-write a portion of Philippians 4:11-12 in the *Remember* column.

RECOGNIZE the lie (in your own words)	REPLACE the lie with truth (in your own words)	REMEMBER the truth (biblical reference)
1.		"I am not saying this because I am in need, for I have learned to be content whatever the circumstances. I know what it is to be in need, and I know what it is to have plenty. I have learned the secret of being content in any and every situation, whether well fed or hungry, whether living in plenty or in want." **Phil. 4:11-12**

RECOGNIZE	REPLACE	REMEMBER
2.		

A spirit of contentment may not come naturally, but making a list of blessings for which you are thankful can be a first step toward a contented attitude. The next step is to thank the Provider for these blessings.

Prayer as the Path to Obedience and Faith

When we thank God for His provision and go to Him in prayer, we are aligning our thoughts with His, trusting His will, and seeking His direction. Jesus promises in Matthew 6:33, that if we seek first His kingdom and His righteousness, all these things will be added to us as well.

Prayer helps us maintain proper priorities and perspective. **And prayer is an integral aspect of our journey toward deeper faith and committed obedience.** Through prayer and the study of His Word, we give God the last word and not the lies of Satan or the frustrations of life.

"Be Still and Know that I Am God."

It was the day after Thanksgiving. We stood to the side of my aunt and uncle's house, the embers from one remaining section of the wreckage, reflecting in my tear-filled eyes. The huddled group ironically shivered in the chill of the morning after such heat had ravaged their home. My ash-stained hands grasped the sooty palms of others as my uncle lifted up a prayer to God—grateful for those who had come to support and gather round in their time of loss.

But neither my tears, nor my uncle's were shed in mourning for the items lost in the fire. His humble and heart-felt emotion was gratefulness for the survival of things that do truly make us happy—the family and friends that surrounded them with their hugs, their prayers, and their strong arms, willing to work to salvage pictures and memories from the remnants of where they had raised their two children, been hospitable to many, and the place they had called home.

Peace and an underlying trust filled my aunt and uncle's hearts at a moment of extreme loss. **Because the source of their happiness was not centered on the contents of the house, but on the Lord who had built the family that resided there.**

Joy was not the only emotion they faced, of course. They went through all of the stages of grief as they mourned the loss of so many of their earthly possessions.

Satan worked on my uncle with the lie, "Now what are you going to do? You've lost everything..." My aunt's biggest struggle was the different ways in which she and my uncle grieved, and handled the losses and rebuilding process. This ushered in the lie that their marriage would not survive. These were two of the many attacks Satan mounted against my aunt and their family in the wake of the tragedy.

Yet, they rejoiced and rested in the fact that God's truths are stronger. My aunt shared, "Through the fourteen months of seeing how the Lord took care of the 'tiniest of details,' I cried more over how sweet God was than over anything that we lost due the fire."

Satan bombarded my aunt with lies about the source of her happiness and her stability, but she clung to verses such as, Isaiah 26:7 and Psalm 46:10, to carry her through when her own strength failed her.

"The path of the righteous is level; you, the Upright One, make the way of the righteous smooth" (Is. 26:7).

"Be still and know that I am God..." (Ps. 46:10).

 On what aspect of God or truth from His Word can you depend when your life situation crumbles around you?

Happiness is *not* the ultimate goal, though Satan works diligently to convince us otherwise. When we respond with faith, we recognize his lies and replace them with truth, remembering the truth from God's Word. Let's give God the **last word on joy** (not happiness based on circumstances), the **last word on obedience** (because God cares more about my holiness than my happiness), and the **last word on priorities** (because when I put Him first, all these things will be added to me as well).

Common Threads

An area in which you'd like to grow or bloom—abounding in faith, hope, and love through truth.

_____

_____

A thorn (lie) you'd like to remove and replace with truth.

_____

_____

An area in which you'd like to dig deeper or need someone to hold you accountable (help to recognize the lie or remember the truth).

_____

_____

A verse or truth to remember that speaks to a lie mentioned in this chapter.

_____

_____

CHAPTER 8

Lie: I Have to Do It on My Own

If you want to go fast, go alone. If you want to go far, go together. – African Proverb

We all want to be great, but we don't want folks to know we want to be great. – Phil Lineberger

Idaho Potato Cake is my favorite. The recipe has been handed down through my family, first located in a *Capper's Weekly* newspaper[7] from my grandma's kitchen in Iowa. It calls for a cup of leftover mashed potatoes and is the moistest chocolate cake you will ever eat.[8]

Now that I have your mouth watering and your mind wondering where is the nearest piece of chocolate, imagine that I only had the cup of mashed potatoes. They may be the creamiest batch of mashed potatoes I have ever made, but without the other

---

[7] Capper, Arthur, pub., "Idaho Potato Cake," *Capper's Weekly*. Topeka, Kansas, 1913-1986. (unknown published date of original recipe)

[8] Idaho Potato Cake recipe available in Appendix A, pg. 261.

ingredients, you will never recognize a cup of cold mashed potatoes as chocolate cake.

So, which is the most important ingredient for making an Idaho Potato cake? Is it the mashed potatoes that determine its uniqueness? Maybe, but they are nothing without the flour, eggs, sugar, and chocolate.

Flour alone is not a cake. Eggs are not a cake. Even combining two or three of the ingredients will not be sufficient for obtaining the desired flavor and texture of Idaho Potato cake.

If I cannot expect one ingredient of the recipe to carry the weight of the full identity of a chocolate cake, how can I expect myself, alone, to carry the full weight of all God has called me to do.

The lie: "I have to do it on my own," is an easy trap for perfectionists, but not one exclusive to their unique challenges. Everyone has a new standard—the Pinterest level of perfection. Pinterest has put added pressure on moms to host a birthday party of Disney World ™ proportions in their backyard. Brides, teachers, cooks, and homeschool moms are each held to a higher level of expectation.

Women are not allowed to admit that we can't do something. We have to be the model sister, wife, mother, aunt, grandmother, student, coworker, and friend—juggling the roles, and all to a Pinterest level of perfection.

My Cry for Help

While spending a week out at a cabin in the mountains of Colorado for concentrated writing on this book, I got snowed in. It was the biggest snow we'd had all season and my front-wheel drive Toyota Corolla and I had enough trouble getting out there. I didn't want to imagine what it would take to make the return trip.

As the snow continued to fall and I enjoyed the beauty of the accumulating white flakes, my worries were also accumulating. The trees, whose branches were laden with snow, bent at the weight of the freshly fallen snow and I was bending at the weight of the magnitude of all I was trying to accomplish.

I had come to the cabin alone and what started as a five-day excursion was quickly turning into a weeklong isolation from civilization. Fear and doubts were rising with each inch of snow and I wondered how I would be able to dig myself out of there.

A strong, independent person who has a hard time asking for help, or admitting when I can't do something—even proud of my abilities—I was crumbling. I had become a basket case, a bundle of nerves, and an emotional wreck. Fear was overtaking and the lies of Satan were overwhelming. I was in the throes of a spiritual battle and I felt like I was losing. It had even become manifest in physical ways by an upset stomach and headache.

I finally picked up the phone, dialed the 33 numbers it took to call someone using a phone card on a landline in an area with no cell service, and my sister answered. I fought through tears and asked if they had plans for the weekend—if it would be possible for them to come help me dig my way out, and follow me in my car back to Denver to make sure I didn't get stuck in the snow or slide on an icy spot in the road.

She listened patiently and compassionately, and committed to talking with her husband and calling me back. Not fifteen minutes later, the phone rang with good news. She had caught her husband on his lunch break and they were going to work out a plan to come and rescue me.

My tears began to flow again—this time, not in the pain of fighting in a spiritual battle, but in thankfulness at God's provision. I had been clinging to the lie that "I have to do it on my own," and it was crippling. And it blinded me from seeing with eyes of hope.

A deeper realization came when they were unable to come and aid me in my return to civilization. **The feeling of relief that had washed over me had come not from receiving the help, but rather in asking for help.** Asking for help was not selfish. It was actually a step toward squelching the prideful stance of the lie that "I have to do it on my own."

Even Jesus asked His disciples for help when He was about to face the most difficult night of His life (Matt. 26:36-41)! He has asked us for help to accomplish the spreading of good news to the ends of the earth (Matt. 28:18-20, Mark 16:15-16).

Our "ever present help in trouble" (Ps. 46:1) liberates us from the bondage of fear when we "lift up [our] eyes to the mountains" and remember the truth that, "[our] help comes from the Lord, the Maker of heaven and earth" (Ps. 121:1-2).

Inspired by my story above, by the lies about doing things on our own, or the lies about asking for help, let's give God the last word and create a Lie/Truth Chart on the next page.

RECOGNIZE the lie (in your own words)	REPLACE the lie with truth (in your own words)	REMEMBER the truth (biblical reference)
1.		
2.		

Israel's Cry for Help

"O our God, will you not judge them? For we have no power to face this vast army that is attacking us. We do not know what to do, but our eyes are upon you" (2 Chron. 20:12).

The Israelites were often oppressed by nearby nations. During the time of the judges, the Midianites were one of their fierce enemies. The Jews cried out to God for deliverance and God heard their cries. So, He called upon Gideon to serve as His instrument of redemption.

Where did God find Gideon (Judg. 6:11)?

 Why was he threshing wheat in the winepress?

The threshing of the wheat normally took place in an open area so that the wheat could be separated from the chaff, but Gideon decided to take on this task in a winepress. He had given up; he was hiding out. He was avoiding the stress and intensity of what was going on around him. And he was afraid.

When the angel of the Lord came to Gideon, he reminded him, "The Lord is with you, mighty warrior" (Judg. 6:12). Gideon doubted, but the Lord affirmed his calling to rescue Israel from Midian's hand three times: once by setting fire to the sacrifice Gideon brought before him and then twice again, per Gideon's request. God made the fleece wet and the ground dry, then made the fleece dry and the ground wet—testimonies that God would save Israel by Gideon's hand.

After God selected Gideon as His vessel for Israel's rescue, what did He tell Gideon in Judges 7:2?

 Why do you think God chose a hesitant, doubtful servant through whom He would bring redemption to His people?

How does God calm Gideon's fears one more time (Judg. 7:8-15)?

List three things that the story of Gideon reveals to us about God's character. (Full story found in Judg. 6-7.)

God most certainly did not leave Gideon to tackle the Midianite army on his own. We see in Judges 6:34, "Then the Spirit of the Lord came upon Gideon..." This is similar language to Galatians 3:27 when we are clothed with Christ through baptism.

 What does it mean to have the Spirit of the Lord upon us or to be clothed with Christ?

With the Spirit of the Lord by our side, we are able to tackle whatever comes our way—not on our own, but with our ever-present help.

Casia's Story

Casia wrestled with the lie that she could tackle whatever God threw at her. Allow me to share part of her story, in her own words:

My heart is suffering from being here on earth. I have this longing in my bones that seems just out of reach. Sometimes I take a bath because I cannot stand the weight of my own body any more. I want to be submerged in water to feel light.

Is it just me? It feels heavy, feels like if only I could look up to the sky and trust the verse that says "look towards things not of this world," I'd rise above it all.

There are days when I feel like Christ gently places His hand under my chin and tilts my head up to see His face. There are days that I feel like I am light, that the weight of my body is not too much... but today, this day when it is raining outside and the gray is seeping into all that had color, I wonder where the sun is. I know it is there. I know that without it all life would cease to exist. It is there just beyond the clouds and in truth it is working harder today to bring me light than it did on that sunny day. It's working harder to break through the clouds to give me life... but it feels just out of reach.

The past year has brought so much unexpected joy and pain. I look back at the journey and wonder what my path would have looked like had I made different decisions.

Would different equal better? I don't believe so.

I would not change one thing, not one decision, not one movement, not one tear. Those tears, decisions, laughs, stillness... it shaped me into this person.

I am being—

Renewed: *To make new, as if new again, to make fresh, strong again.*

I have gone through this before with God a few years ago, and I'm sure it won't be the last time. God promised to never leave me or abandon me until His work is complete in me. I am walking the journey with Him trusting that to be true. Have you been here? When all you thought you knew falls away and you realize that you have been dictating to God what you believe you have to have for your safety?

This is my thorn in my side: I am strong, I am competent, I can love You with all that I have in me. "Come on God, throw it at me! I'll show You what I'm made of!"

I have believed the lie that I, "Casia," can conquer anything God throws at me. Can you see the lie in that? I believe that God is in fact throwing things at me just to see if I can withstand the pressure. And when I believe that, I take all the power of the cross, all the pain, sacrifice, and blood shed for me and I put Jesus back in the ground.

He did not DIE for me, go through HELL, be beat and spit on, be abandoned by everyone He loved, be separated from God, to then just throw trials at me to see how strong I am.

Let's ponder what it meant for Jesus to be separated from God for just a moment. He had NEVER, up until that point, been without God. For eternity they were one. We have no way to even begin to comprehend the magnitude of pain, loss, sadness, and agony that They must have felt— maybe you could compare it to losing all movement of your body, knowing what you were but only left with what you are not... That only scratches the surface of the sacrifice He made.

The second lie is that I have to be strong. This lie goes back 30 years and is so deep that its roots wrap themselves around every fiber of my being. It is so thoroughly woven into who I am that I can be staring at it right in the face and not even see it.

Just the other day as I lay in bed weeping, the Holy Spirit met me there in my sadness.

Me: "I can't do this, I can't hold it all up, I'm tired."

The sweet Holy Spirit: "Casia, you don't have to. Let it go. We have it. We have you."

Me: "But this is who I am! It's what I do! I am strong!"

Holy Spirit: "You are strong, but not because you have held things together. You are strong because We are with you. REST."

Well if you take that away from me then what am I left with? My strength defines me or I thought it did. But it doesn't define me. The reality is that I didn't cave in on myself after having to leave Africa, or ending my engagement because it was not healthy, but because the Trinity was with me, not because I have enough strength to get myself through it.

And the flip side of that... I was blessed by God with an amazing husband who loves me so well not because I was willing to sacrifice and trust God. He blessed me with Phil because that is who God is. He blesses because He is love. It is not a about "If I give God something, He'll give me a blessing." Rather, it is a hand in hand, walking together through the good and the bad.

So I can't stand the weight of myself right now, because I have seen the sin that has been lurking under my skin. I am giving it up so that I can be renewed. That process is hard but so good. It is exhausting to try and hold a world together that is riddled with hurt. **I am letting God unwrap the lie that I have to be strong, but that hurts, and truth has to be put on those bare places so they can heal.** *I'm looking to the Sun.*

"I remember the moment You breathed on my small heart, Your voice was a whisper at the foot of my bed. The room washed in yellow, the sun of a new day. I sang with my eyes closed. I wasn't afraid." Lauren Plank Goans[9]

The Support of the Holy Spirit

 What role did the Holy Spirit play in Casia's story?

Four times in the book of John, the Greek word, *paraclete* is used to describe the Holy Spirit. It is most often translated as

---

[9] Plank Goans, Lauren. Singer, songwriter friend of Casia

Counselor, but the same Greek word is used in 1 John 2:1 to describe Jesus as our Advocate.

 What is the promise given by Christ about the Holy Spirit in John 14:16-17, 26?

According to Gordon Dalbey in *Healing the Masculine Soul,* the Greek word *paraclete* was an ancient warrior's term. "Greek soldiers went into battle in pairs," says Dalbey, "so when the enemy attacked, they could draw together, back-to-back, covering each other's blind side. One's battle partner was the paraclete."[10]

A *paraclete* **stays by our side, counsels us, comforts us, advocates for us, and is a battle-ready partner through whatever we face.**

Now, let's look two chapters later about how Jesus describes the Spirit's role. Read John 16:7-15. What does the Spirit speak (v. 13)?

Let's give the Advocate, our *paraclete* and speaker of truth the last word!

---

[10] Dalbey, Gordon. *Healing the Masculine Soul* (Nashville: Thomas Nelson, 2003) 124-5.

The Support of the Church

God not only gave us the Holy Spirit as a helper and one who walks by our side, but He also gave us His church.

The challenge is: Satan wants to do all he can to hinder us from tapping into the resources that God provides.

He tells us that we are a failure if we ask for help, just like he did with me in the mountains and with Josephine, whose story I share below.

Josephine[11] drove her Camaro from California, halfway across the country to attend college. The university setting, away from family and friends, was a stressful transition.

"I began to withdraw socially. At first, it was an unconscious decision. I avoided the cafeteria, telling myself I had no time for lunch or dinner because I needed to study or practice my music. Overwhelmed with the new homework load and feeling quite out of my comfort zone, I found excuses not to socialize or eat.

"Eventually, it became difficult to eat in public. No red flags went off in my mind. If days had gone by and I was physically weak, I would tell myself that I didn't have time for a sit-down meal and would drive through somewhere quickly, constantly checking the rearview mirror, afraid that someone might catch me eating. Still no red flags."

One Monday afternoon, on a segment of Oprah about eating disorders, a woman walked through her "normal" day. Josephine said, "It was like looking in a mirror. That was the moment I realized I had a problem, but I was already so conditioned in my thought patterns and behaviors, I didn't know how to get out of it."

---

[11] Name changed per the contributor's request

Asking for help was a new concept since life had been somewhat idyllic up to that point. She now felt out of control and drowning in loneliness. "I was moody (not eating will do that to you), and kept busy studying in order to avoid the real problem.

"I could have asked for help. People cared. An acquaintance from back home went to school with me there. He was my only friend, really, and having seen the dramatic change from high school to college, he tried to intervene. He would call me most nights after curfew and invite me to lunch the next day. Every night, I would accept, but when the time came for me to eat a meal with him, I would become insecure about whether he was judging my portion sizes or calculating my calorie intake—men, by the way, don't think that deeply.

"I often initiated an argument with my only friend and walked away angry for the sake of not having to eat in public. Every night, he would call and check up on me, I would apologize, and he'd say, "Want to try again tomorrow?" He was a friend when I didn't deserve one."

Josephine spent the entire year starving herself, isolating, and living under the lie that she had everything under control. She never let anyone know what life was really like.

"Admitting I needed help, in my mind at the time, meant failure."

"My future was unknown territory. I had spent my whole life with a plan and that plan was unraveling. My anxiety got the best of me, and my mind transformed into needing to control the only thing I could: my diet."

Josephine's vocal coach was the one that forced her hand. The coach noticed weakness, stress in her voice, and a change in behavior. Counseling was a difficult, but necessary step if she wanted to stay in school. The counselor encouraged her to talk with her parents, in spite of her fear of disappointing or worrying them.

Fast-forward two healthy years later. Josephine was traveling the world, getting involved in mission trips, and using her second language for God's kingdom. She loved her life, but it was a battle won, not the war.

"Satan never gives up the fight. When my schedule got too busy, or when some guy dumped me, I would have trouble with my old behaviors and damaging thoughts. It caused me, at times, to be either very shy or too forward with men. I regret that too. I was looking for approval when I already had God's.

"Satan lied when he tried to convince me that I must have all the answers now. He lied when he sent me the message that I was a failure if I asked for help—that's what a church family is for! He lied when he tried to tell me I was not good enough. I am perfectly and wonderfully made!

"Nowadays, I let my good Christian friends know when I need prayers. I seek out professional help from time to time when I need it. Satan never stops fighting and neither will I, but I no longer fight alone. The verse that has always been there and helped me to remember who is in the driver's seat is Psalm 4:8. It's a simple verse, but for someone like me to give it over to God every night and lie down in peace, knowing that He makes me to dwell in safety, it is a huge one."

"In peace I will lie down and sleep, for you alone, Lord, make me dwell in safety" (Ps. 4:8).

Before we continue, make a Lie/Truth Chart on the next page, inspired by Josephine, as she continues to give God the last word in her life.

RECOGNIZE the lie (in your own words)	REPLACE the lie with truth (in your own words)	REMEMBER the truth (biblical reference)

One Another

Over fifty times in the New Testament, God gives us instructions about how to interact with **one another**. The church is a body with Christ as the head (1 Cor. 12) and we support **each other** as each part does its work (Eph. 4:11-16).

"Carry **each other's** burdens, and in this way you will fulfill the law of Christ" (Gal. 6:2).

"Therefore confess your sins to **each other** and pray for **each other** so that you may be healed. The prayer of a righteous person is powerful and effective" (James 5:16).

"And let us consider how we may spur **one another** on toward love and good deeds" (Heb. 10:24).

"Be devoted to **one another** in love. Honor **one another** above yourselves" (Rom. 12:10).

We usually do this at the end of the chapter, but I want to give special emphasis to the Common Threads now, as we put some of these verses into practice. The Common Threads are a way of making personal and practical many of the points we have discussed regarding the lie of "I Have to Do It on My Own."

In light of all of the verses about relationship, we must first be willing to engage in relationship—step out of our comfort zones and into other people's lives.

You may feel hesitant to ask for help. A past experience may have given you some trust issues...

Pray that God will lead you to the right person with whom you can be vulnerable. As we discussed in chapter 6, Satan wants to trap us in the lie that we are alone and that there is no one that understands what we have been through.

However, even when we feel that the church and others fail us, we have a Perfect Paraclete—a battle-ready, time-tested, Advocate, and Counselor by our side.

So, as you share the Common Threads with your Iron Rose Sisters, don't forget to lift each other up in prayer and invite the Holy Spirit, our spiritual paraclete, to support you and give you hope.

Special Note: This is NOT the end of the chapter just because we are looking at the Common Threads now.

Common Threads

 An area in which you'd like to grow or bloom—abounding in faith, hope, and love through truth.

_____

_____

A thorn (lie) you'd like to remove and replace with truth.

_____

_____

An area in which you'd like to dig deeper or need someone to hold you accountable (help to recognize the lie or remember the truth).

_____

_____

A verse or truth to remember that speaks to a lie mentioned in this chapter.

_____

_____

Strength Through Christ

Write out Philippians 4:13 below:

Read the verse several times out loud and each time, pause after a different word, reflecting on what they each mean...

Go back and circle the word "through." What happens when you emphasize that part of the verse?

It is not about being able to accomplish any and every thing we want to because Christ is with us. It is, rather, about having the strength to face whatever comes our way because we are in Christ.

 How does our reaction to life's circumstances alter when we consider the two different interpretations of Philippians 4:13?

When we accomplish things through Christ, we no longer have to face anything alone. What does Matthew 11:28-29 say about that truth?

Easy Traps with the Lie: I Have to Do It on My Own

Comparison Lie: I can't do this as well as someone else, so why would I even try.

Overwhelmed Lie: This situation is hopeless and I see no way out.

Prideful Lie: I'm the best at doing this.

Selfish Lie: I can't let anyone help with this project (or let her use her gifts to serve).

Worry Lie: The more I worry; the better I can fix things.

Using the personal lies you face (possibly one of those listed above), select three of the following truths from the Bible (or choose your own) to create a Lie/Truth Chart, giving God the last word of hope.

Exodus 14:14

Psalm 63:6-8

Deuteronomy 8:4

1 Samuel 17:45-47

Jeremiah 32:27

1 Corinthians 12:12-14

Colossians 3:16

RECOGNIZE the lie (in your own words)	REPLACE the lie with truth (in your own words)	REMEMBER the truth (biblical reference)
1.		
2.		

RECOGNIZE	REPLACE	REMEMBER
3.		

In closing, let's look at one more example of God's design for one-another fellowship and the support of others.

Read Exodus 17:8-16.

What did God provide for Moses when his hands grew tired?

If you are like Moses, feeling weak, pray that God will lead you to an Aaron and Hur who can support you. **There is hope and God will not allow you to face the battle alone.**

If, however, you are in a time of strength, pray that God can use you as an Aaron or Hur in someone else's life to bring her hope and remind her of truth.

Two are better than one,

> *because they have a good return for their labor:*

If either of them falls down,

> *one can help the other up.*

But pity anyone who falls

> *and has no one to help them up.*

Also, if two lie down together, they will keep warm.

But how can one keep warm alone?

Though one may be overpowered,

two can defend themselves.

A cord of three strands is not quickly broken. (Eccl. 4:9-12)

A man asked his young son to break a bundle of sticks. He returned a little later to find the lad frustrated in the task. He has raised the bundle high and smashed it on his knee, but he only bruised his knee. He had set the bundle against a wall and stomped hard with his foot, but the bundle barely bent.

The father took the bundle from the child and untied it. Then he began to break the sticks easily—one at a time. [12]

So it is with the church: united we are strong, divided we can fail or be broken. Let's give God the last word and replace the lie, "I Have to Do It on My Own."

---

[12] Green, Michael P., ed., *1500 Illustrations for Biblical Teaching* (Grand Rapids: Baker Books, 2005), 66.

CHAPTER 9

Lies We Believe When We're Discouraged

Sometimes God calms the storm—and sometimes he lets the storm rage and calms his child. – Unknown

What we do in the crisis always depends on whether we see the difficulties in the light of God, or God in the shadow of the difficulties. – G. Campbell Morgan

Earth hath no sorrow that heaven cannot heal. – Thomas Moore

E very year, sometime after Thanksgiving and before Christmas, there are three movies I traditionally watch: *Miracle on 34th Street*,[13] *Elf*,[14] and Frank Capra's *It's a Wonderful Life*[15] with Jimmy Stewart. *It's a Wonderful Life* is a classic and no matter how many times I watch it, I tear up at the outpouring of love and support for George Bailey at the end.

---

[13] Twentieth Century Fox Film Corporation, 1994.

[14] New Line Cinema, 2003.

[15] Liberty Films, 1946.

At the very beginning of the movie, the angel, Clarence, says to the angel, Joseph, both represented by stars in the night sky:

"You sent for me, sir?"

"Yes, Clarence. A man down on earth needs our help."

"Splendid! Is he sick?"

"No. Worse. He's discouraged."

Did you catch that? I've seen the movie countless times, but that line caught my attention in a way it never had before. "No. Worse. He's discouraged."

Discouragement is debilitating. It is game changing. It creates a watered-down version of who we truly are. Do you already feel your shoulders sagging as some of those discouraging thoughts come to mind?

Discouragement is one of the most basic realities of life, but one that can make us feel guilty (a concept we will explore in the next chapter) or lead us into depression. Yes, I said the "D-word." But if we can't talk about it with our Christian sisters, with whom do we expect to tackle the challenges faced by us or other loved ones we know? Depression brings us to our knees in desperation and in prayer. And for those without the hope of Christ, depression and discouragement sink to an entirely different depth.

Depression affects our memory—how we recall things that have happened, what people have said, even how we felt at the time. It also affects our mental processing and clarity. Do you not think that Satan would take advantage while we are down, exploit our affected memories, and prefer to keep us entrapped in lies?

What a low-down, dirty, rotten scoundrel! And he is! **The father of lies shows no mercy and pounces when we are already vulnerable.** If there is ever a time for truth of an abundant life filled with hope, it is when we are discouraged or depressed. Let's not give merit to the lies, but rather give God the last word!

Elijah's Battle with Depression

Elijah battled the same kind of lies right after he had tasted tremendous victory at God's hand. **His despair invited the discouraging thoughts to fade his memory and overshadow God's promises.**

 Summarize in three sentences what happened in 1 Kings 18:16-46.

What does Elijah say in 1 Kings 19:4?

When/Why was Elijah overcome by these thoughts (1 Kings 19:1-3)?

What happened next (1 Kings 19:5-10)?

Describe Elijah's state of mind as he slept in the cave of Horeb, the mountain of God, after forty days and forty nights of travel. What kind of thoughts and lies were whirling in his head that night?

Continue reading the rest of the story in 1 Kings 19:11-21.

God's Loving Response to Elijah

We are going to explore the five ways God responds to Elijah's depression and the depth of pain in his soul.

➤ God took care of Elijah's physical needs.

➤ God affirmed Elijah by making His presence known.

➤ God gave Elijah a task.

➤ God reminded Elijah of truth.

➤ And God provided assistance, reminding Elijah that he wasn't alone.

In the space provided after each of God's five responses on the previous page, elaborate on how God did each of those things for Elijah, including the biblical reference from 1 Kings 19.

 What is your reaction to God's provision for Elijah?

Does God do the same for us today? How so or how not?

(Bonus Reflection: Why did God not just carry Elijah off in a chariot of fire at that moment, and save him the added misery?)

God Responds in Our Time of Despair

 Let's be specific about how God provides in our discouraged and depressed times today. In the space below, give at least one example of how God Himself, or through His church, responds in the exact same ways He did for Elijah when we are down in the depths.

➢ God takes care of our physical needs.

➢ God affirms us by making His presence known.

➢ God gives us a task.

➢ God reminds us of truth.

➢ And God provides assistance, reminding us that we are not alone.

As we discussed in chapter 6: Lie: I Am Alone, God has blessed us with Christian sisters, or Iron Rose Sisters, that can serve as iron sharpening iron, encouraging and inspiring us to be as beautiful as a rose in spite of a few thorns. I know that one of the thorns I have faced is depression. **And I am grateful to God for the Iron Rose Sisters He has put in my life that have blessed me in the same ways that God responded to Elijah's needs.**

Dark Days of My Soul

Many of us, like Elijah, have experienced dark times. Statistically speaking, almost twice as many women as men will face a time of depression during their lifetime. "Biological, life cycle, hormonal, and psychosocial factors that women experience may be linked to women's higher depression rate."[16] Oh, those lovely hormones that complicate the issue and affect our brain chemistry, especially when we get our period, are pregnant, give birth, and go through menopause. Ten to fifteen percent of women will battle post-partum depression after giving birth.[16]

Between six and seven percent of the U.S. population in any given year will report a major depressive episode. This does not include ongoing battles with depression or unreported depression, which is more common than those that seek help for their depression.[16]

This makes it difficult to ascertain exactly how many people have faced at least one depressive episode at some point in their lives, but these statistics affirm that it is definitely a common struggle. Some people are more susceptible to it, but research is still unclear about why it affects some people and not others.

Whether or not you have personally fought depression, I guarantee that someone close to you has or will struggle with depression. I say this not to discourage you, but rather to prepare you and to give you hope as someone who can speak personally from the other side of depression. **Together, we can give God the last word when assaulted by the lies compounded by depression.**

From Psalm 91: *"He who dwells in the shelter (covering, hiding place) of the Most High, will rest in the shadow of the Almighty. I will say of the Lord: He is my refuge and my fortress, my God, in whom I*

---

[16] National Institute of Mental Health, NIMH, · www.nimh.org Additional resources from the National Institute of Mental Health are available in **Appendix B**, including a list of symptoms, and ways to help a loved one or yourself through depression.

trust... He will cover you with his feathers, and under his wings will you find refuge; his faithfulness will be your shield and rampart. You will not fear the terror of night, nor the arrow that flies by day..."

Valley Time

While I could share from some of my personal experience, please allow my friend, Sherry to describe her own situation near the end of 2009.

I was in a very dark place. There were battles on every front and I felt as though I was losing every battle. One day I decided I didn't want to fight anymore. I was tired. I packed a bag and placed it in the trunk of my car while no one in my household was present. Later in the day I announced I was running an errand when in actuality I was running away. I did not tell my husband or my closest friends where I was going. The truth is I did not know myself.

My first stop was the Grist Mill at Stone Mountain Park (Atlanta, Georgia). It was one of my favorite places to retreat and pray, and so I did. I stayed at the park for a couple of hours pleading with God for reprieve from the battle. While I was vigorously waving a white flag, it was as though it was waved in front of blind eyes. I was plummeting deeper into darkness.

It was decision time but I did not like the choices I was giving myself. I decided the safest decision was to give myself more time away from every person and every responsibility. I sent a text to my husband telling him I was fine but I still needed some time alone. He was very gracious. It was at that point I turned off my cell phone and I checked into a hotel. By the time I got to my room my voice mailbox had several messages from my husband and from one of my dearest friends. It was a couple of hours before I could listen to the messages and a while longer until I could respond. What words did I have to explain my behavior? None.

In their writings, both Oswald Chambers and C.S. Lewis describe something called the Dark Night of the Soul. They could write about it because it was their experience at one time or another in their own lives. It certainly describes my experience too. If you are like me you often equate darkness with evil and that does not bode well with this Christ-follower. The truth is even in my darkest moment, and in His silence, I sensed the presence of God or as I have since described it, the Shadow of God.

David paints the picture well in Psalm 23:

"The LORD is my shepherd, I shall not be in want. He makes me lie down in green pastures, he leads me beside quiet waters, and he restores my soul. He guides me in paths of righteousness for his name's sake. Even though I walk through the valley of the shadow of death, I will fear no evil, for YOU ARE WITH ME; your rod and staff they comfort me."

On that day several years ago, God had not abandoned me. Looking back now I can see He made incredible provision. In the valley, He gave me a quiet place to lie down, His presence, and His Word and Spirit to guide me out of the valley and to a much better place. His faithfulness then is all I need now to remind me that any valley-time I face is still proof of His love.

 What would Sherry's Lie/Truth Chart look like?

RECOGNIZE the lie (in your own words)	REPLACE the lie with truth (in your own words)	REMEMBER the truth (biblical reference)

Satan Hits Us When We're Down

As you can imagine, Satan longs to take advantage of the times when we are down. He adds insult to injury. He bombards us with lies that are even easier to believe when we are discouraged or depressed.

Satan provides excuses to not seek help. He attacks insecurities, isolates us from family, friends, and church. He undermines our self-worth, and distorts the truths we once held dear. **And an especially enticing lie Satan uses when we're down: That truth applies to everyone but me.**

However, we can equip ourselves with tools to proclaim and cling to truth in those dark days of the soul.

Why, my soul, are you downcast?

Why so disturbed within me?

Put your hope in God,

for I will yet praise him,

my Savior and my God.

My soul is downcast within me;

therefore I will remember you

from the land of the Jordan,

the heights of Hermon—from Mount Mizar.

Deep calls to deep

in the roar of your waterfalls;

all your waves and breakers

have swept over me.

By day the Lord directs his love,

at night his song is with me—

a prayer to the God of my life. (Ps. 42:5-8)

Recognizing God's Voice

Elijah recognized God's voice as a whisper (1 Kings 19:12-13). The sheep recognized and followed the voice of the Good Shepherd (John 10:2-5). **It's about knowing God, not just about Him, in order to recognize His voice of truth in the midst of trying times.**

The more time we spend in the Word, the more we come to know His words, and the easier it is to discern His words of truth amidst the bombardment of lies.

My sister and brother-in-law were on a camping trip outside of cell range. But our other housemate needed to reach them in order to ask permission to bring home a puppy she wanted to adopt.

"Michelle! I can't reach Kim and Paxton and I really want to bring this puppy home!" Shannon proceeded to describe the dog, and then went into her rapid-fire questions. "I need to know what you think they would say. I don't want to get it and have it at the house without their permission, but there is no way the puppy will still be here tomorrow. It'll only be like two weeks because, after that, I move out, and we'll be headed home for our wedding... What do I do?!"

I considered Shannon's predicament and responded, "I hate to speak for them, but I understand you really want the dog and want to at least check with someone who knows them well." I continued with a few points that I thought they would make, and things that should be taken into consideration, like how their own dogs would respond.

Shannon thanked me and was going to try and call them one more time, but had decided that she would probably go ahead and get the puppy…

A couple of hours later, I met Shannon and her fiancé at the house to help introduce the puppy to my sister and brother-in law's dogs. After the dogs' initial introductions, Shannon looked at me, surprised.

"I forgot to tell you. I was able to reach Kim on the phone and ask her about the puppy. She mentioned every single one of the things you said she would. Some of the things she said were verbatim what you said!"

I smiled and responded, "Well, we kind of know each other." Sisters, living in the same house, conversing, spending time together… I didn't want to speak for her, but I felt confident that I would represent her to the best of my ability because I knew her and I knew her voice.

May we come to know God's voice so intimately!

Satan's lies scream in attack. God's voice is a gentle whisper of comfort and hope in the midst of the storm. When we listen for God's voice and are attentive to His words of truth, Satan's clamoring is quieted. And God gets the last word.

 List three ways in which we can come to know God's voice more intimately. Circle the one that you most need to work on.

Battle on All Fronts

When we are in the throes of any battle, it is vital to hear and follow our Commander's voice. It is the only way to give Him the last word in all of the areas in which Satan attacks.

Satan wages battle on all fronts: mental, emotional, physical, and spiritual.

When discouraged, our problems can overshadow the presence of God. However, when we are intimately connected with Him, His presence outshines the darkness.

 Why is it important to let God's presence outshine the darkness?

Discouragement and depression are like dark shadows—a weight that we cannot easily shake and that threaten to overwhelm. They pervade every facet of our lives: physical, mental, emotional, and spiritual. And so why would Satan not also want to interject his lying tongue in each of those areas?

Satan's **physical attacks** may have to do with self-image, health, weight, a loss of possessions…

Mental attacks can take the form of doubts regarding self-worth, unclear thinking, a clouded memory, or forgetting God's provision in the past.

Emotional attacks: resurgence of insecurities from our past, new fears and worries, or attacks on our family members that affect us emotionally as well.

And no matter which of the other kinds of attacks Satan uses, they all become a form of **spiritual attack** because of the way they affect our relationship with God. They discourage us from believing the truth, found in His Word, which cuts through Satan's lying attacks, and gives God the last word. Satan tries to shake our faith, squelch our hope, and distance us from God's love. We are in a spiritual battle (Eph. 6:10-18)!

Choose one of the areas in which Satan is currently attacking you personally with his lies, placing it in the Lie/Truth Chart below (physical, mental, emotional, or spiritual attacks). Don't forget to replace the lie with truth and remember the truth through scripture.

RECOGNIZE the lie (in your own words)	REPLACE the lie with truth (in your own words)	REMEMBER the truth (biblical reference)
Physical attack/lie		
Mental attack/lie		
Emotional attack/lie		

RECOGNIZE	REPLACE	REMEMBER
Spiritual attack/lie		

Each of these lies are intensified when we are already discouraged in another area of our life. When facing depression, mental fog and negative thinking are classic symptoms that Satan capitalizes on.

Revealing the Lie When It Seems Like the Truth

The truth is still the truth, even if it is clouded by doubt. Do the objects in a room change their form when the light is turned off? No! And we are reminded of their shape when we turn on the light.

It's like when you stub your toe in the middle of the night. The bedpost did not randomly move. Nor was it the intent of that rogue pair of shoes to trip you up on your way to the bathroom. Under the cover of dark and the stupor of sleep, nothing is clear and everything is malicious.

A young child, afraid of the dark, will imagine all sorts of things lurking in the shadows. But his trust in mom and dad allows them to have the last word, instead of his fears. He allows them to reveal the truth of what is hidden in the shadows, and that truth allows him to rest, peaceful in the hope of their loving protection.

God is light and in Him is no darkness at all—not even a shadow (1 John 1:5). Nor does He change like shifting shadows (James 1:17). Therefore, we can always rely on His unchanging nature and His light to cut through the darkness—to reveal the truth and dispel the lie.

The gospel of John speaks more than any of the other gospels about the nature of truth and Christ as the embodiment of that truth. In 1 John, the author clarifies those truths as life, light, love, and faith as beloved children of God.

 Read John 8:12 and John 14:6. How does it encourage you to know that Jesus is light and truth when you are discouraged?

Encouraging One Another

God and His truth are our ultimate sources of encouragement, but, as we highlighted in chapter 8, He has also given us the church as an instrument through which we can be encouraged and encourage others. And don't forget the blessing of encouragement from our Iron Rose Sisters!

Discourage: lack of courage

Encourage: to instill with courage

 How can someone best instill *you* with courage?

List five concrete, specific ways in which you can encourage someone else (you might refer back to the ways in which God encouraged Elijah, as we discussed earlier in this chapter).

Put a star next to the one that you can put into practice this week.

As I am sure you mentioned, **two of the best ways to encourage someone who is facing a difficult time are prayer and Scripture.** In addition to what you starred above, I encourage you to send someone a card letting her know that you are praying for her and her family. Be sure to include an encouraging verse that you have written out.

We have a choice when we are discouraged. We can have a pity party, or a time of counting our blessings, seeking words filled with hope. And in the same way that I was able to speak for my sister Kim because I knew her voice, **we can represent God's voice of truth in the lives of others because we know Him and have heard His words.**

"May the God of hope fill you with all joy and peace as you trust in him, so that you may overflow with hope by the power of the Holy Spirit" (Rom. 15:13).

Make a list of seven blessings you can count from this past week, or things for which you are grateful. (You can keep it simple or be elaborate. For example, "water" is always top on my list!)

You're Not the Only One

When we are discouraged or depressed, it is easy to lose sight of hope, especially if sin is involved. **Depression is not a sin, but it can be caused by sin,** like David's depression caused by the guilt of his adultery (1 Sam. 11-12). **Or depression can engage us in a spiritual battle,** like it did for Hannah when she cried out to God year after year for a son. The prophet, Eli, even thought she was drunk (1 Sam. 1).

Naomi's bitterness of soul caused her to want to be called Mara (which means bitter) instead of Naomi, after she had lost her husband and two sons (Ruth 1). There was a definite spiritual battle in the dark days of her soul, as she had lost all hope.[17]

What about Christ Himself? Read Luke 22:39-46.

---

[17] A supplementary list of biblical examples of depression and biblical answers to depression and discouragement are included with the resources in Appendix C.

What evidence do we see of Christ's overwhelming discouragement?

 Name two things Jesus did to combat His discouragement from Luke 22.

Prayer and Praise

"When my life was ebbing away, I remembered you, Lord, and my prayer rose to you, to your holy temple" (Jonah 2:7).

Prayer and praise are keys to remembering truth at all times, but especially when we are discouraged. They can each feel like we are going through the motions when our heart is not in it. Yet, **prayer and praise are powerful vessels of hope that transform our perspective from darkness to light, from a lack of courage to encouragement, through remembering the truth.** Prayer and praise give God the last word instead of the thoughts that whirl inside our own heads.

 What roles have prayer and praise played in your life? This is a good time to share a story of how they uplifted you or filled you with hope when you were discouraged.

Prayer and praise help me focus on the presence of God instead of the presence of my problems.

Words of Hope: God is Faithful

In closing this chapter, I would like to share some excerpts from my prayer journal during a time when I personally faced intense depression caused by a traumatic event (a broken engagement), coupled with the decision to launch Iron Rose Sister Ministries (IRSM). The rug had been yanked out from under my neatly planned-out future. And while I felt God's assurance of the clear vision He had given me to start IRSM, the unknowns in my future were more overwhelming and daunting than those assurances. **The depression clouded my ability to remember the truth.** Yet I clung to Scripture and God provided Iron Rose Sisters and family to remind me of truth.

Notice my wrestling between lies and truth. I was shocked to re-read these entries and reflect on God's light of hope and my longing to give Him the last word in the midst of my pain and confusion.

In light of the initial decision to take the leap of faith to launch IRSM, I was "100% excited and 100% scared." I lost count of the times that I mentioned being scared in my prayer journal, but there were also statements like, "I trust You to meet all my needs according to Your glorious riches in Christ Jesus" (from Phil 4:19).

"I'm on an emotional roller coaster and want to get off. I read the Scriptures and am reminded of Your sovereignty and provision, but reality also slaps me in the face."

~~~~

"I'm not handling the stress well and I fear it will get worse before it gets better. It feels like a vicious, never-ending cycle that I can't seem to get right or have anything work out as a blessing without additional stress.

I can't do it. Even my attempts to ask for help keep backfiring or adding more frustration, sadness, or stress.

I'm giving it all to You—more than I can even put on paper. It's all Yours.

Please give me wisdom and strength and guide my steps. Please also return my health to me."

~~~~

"You may very well be delighting in the fact that I say I can't do any of it because then You get to show up big-time and You get all the glory. Go for it! Because I know I can't."

~~~~

"I'm so overwhelmed, exhausted, angry, emotional and a lot of other things. Last night, my prayers were groans. I couldn't even write: Refiner's fire. Rescuer—but when?"

~~~~

"Please help me know where to start and then move forward with it all. One step at a time, one day at a time, right? Each day has enough trouble of its own" (Matt. 6:34).

The truths from Scripture that I had hidden in my heart came back to me and strengthened me, even if, at the time, I didn't make note of the book, chapter, and verse. But do you see how Satan tried to take advantage and intensify my doubts and insecurities when I was already discouraged?

Inspired by the excerpts from my prayer journal, use the blank Lie/Truth Chart below to recognize a lie, replace it with truth, and remember the truth—giving God the last word when you are discouraged.

RECOGNIZE the lie (in your own words)	REPLACE the lie with truth (in your own words)	REMEMBER the truth (biblical reference)

Don't forget to save some time with your Iron Rose Sisters to pray together over the Common Threads and praise God for how He is working in your lives to recognize the lies, replace them with truth, and remember the truth, thus filling us with hope.

Common Threads

 An area in which you'd like to grow or bloom—abounding in faith, hope, and love through truth.

A thorn (lie) you'd like to remove and replace with truth.

_____

_____

An area in which you'd like to dig deeper or need someone to hold you accountable (help to recognize the lie or remember the truth).

_____

_____

A verse or truth to remember that speaks to a lie mentioned in this chapter.

_____

_____

This is a good week to refer to the Blank Lie/Truth Chart (pg. 293) at the back of the book that you can use as a reference when you are discouraged, when Satan attacks, or when the lies threaten. This way we can always be filled with hope and remember to give God the last word!

CHAPTER 10

Lie: God is Punishing Me for My Past

Conscience is merely your own judgment of the right or wrong of our actions, and so can never be a safe guide unless enlightened by the word of God. – Tryon Edwards

Do not expect God to cover what you are not willing to uncover. – Duncan Campbell

"My son got diabetes and died from complications of the disease because God was punishing me for marrying a non-Christian... I've made so many bad decisions in my life that there is no way God wants to hear from me. I feel like I can't talk to Him because I know He won't listen to me."

This was not a statement I expected to hear from a seventy-two year old woman, one who had been a Christian for years, but who was letting Satan have the last word.

Humbled by the scenario before me, I thanked God for the opportunity to speak words of truth and freedom into this sister's life. She had been living her entire life entrapped by Satan's lies, burdened by guilt.

I began, "You have three grown children, right?" A loving glimmer filled her eyes and she responded in the affirmative.

"And, even today, when one of your kids is in trouble or has done something wrong, do you want them to avoid you or come to you so that you can comfort them, advise them, and show them love?"

"Well, of course I want them to come to me!"

"And do you think that our loving Heavenly Father is any different when one of His children messes up? Don't you think He longs to comfort us, advise us, and shower us with His love?"

"I've never thought of it that way before..."

The following Sunday, upon greeting my friend, her face was one of peace and she looked as if she had lost 100 pounds off her already small frame. The joy stemming from her newfound freedom was unquenchable. **She had embraced the truth of God's abounding love, giving *Him* the last word in her life.**

Satan's Trap of Guilt

Satan wants to rob us of the abundant life Christ offers (John 10:10), but there is hope for redemption, freedom, forgiveness, and even a clean conscience! Shame and guilt do not have to define our lives and our relationships.

Satan creates a negative filter through which we see our actions and decisions. We become focused on our sin and unworthiness instead of the grace and forgiveness that God offers.

Even if we have intellectually accepted God's forgiveness, it can be hard to forgive ourselves, especially on an emotional level. **The shame we feel from our past sins overshadows the cleansing power of God's grace.**

God's forgiveness is real and redeeming. When He buys us back, the slate is washed clean. We are able to start anew.

" 'Come now, let us settle the matter,' says the Lord. 'Though your sins are like scarlet, they shall be white as snow; though they are red as crimson, they shall be like wool'" (Isa. 1:18).

How does God refer to Israel in Jeremiah 31:4, 21-22?

 What does it mean for God to refer to Israel as a virgin?

Throughout the Old Testament, God compares His relationship with Israel to a marriage, with Israel being the unfaithful bride. He has Hosea marry Gomer, an adulterous woman, as a direct parallel of Israel's adulterous relationship with God (Hosea 3:1-3). Other prophets remind Israel of God's faithfulness in spite of their infidelity.

However, in the prophetic words of Jeremiah, God welcomes Israel to a level of redemption that totally wipes the slate clean. "Virgin Israel" offers more than mere forgiveness.

Redemption is being bought back, but a reference to "Virgin Israel" is about being brought back to a condition before any infidelity. Can virginity and innocence be reclaimed? In God's eyes and according to His invitation, it can!

But His redemption is not an invitation to go on sinning that His grace may increase (Rom. 6:1). If we got what we deserved, death would be our only option (Rom. 6:23).

God's Complete Forgiveness

After betrayal by a friend, trust is broken; the relationship falters on a shaky foundation in an attempt to take steps forward and mend the brokenness. As failed and flawed human beings, we recognize that things may never return to their original condition—whether broken or strengthened, it will never be the same. One cannot glue back together a broken vase and restore its original, unblemished beauty.

But God can! **Our relationship with God can be reinstated to its original, unblemished beauty.**

And that statement is beyond our comprehension. It is as simple and as complex as Jesus explaining to Nicodemus about being born again in John 3.

Guilt and shame hinder us from accepting the generous blessing God offers for total and unparalleled redemption, through repentance and obedience. Satan uses whatever tools in his arsenal to prevent us from understanding or accepting God's gift of complete forgiveness.

Israel also struggled to grasp this truth—an understandable confusion when we look to certain Old Testament stories. Under the old covenant, God often exacted immediate punishment on the guilty. We tremble in fear at stories like that of Uzzah who was struck down after reaching out to catch the ark of the covenant when the oxen stumbled (2 Sam. 6:6-7). Fire consumed Aaron's sons, Nadab and Abihu, after they offered unauthorized fire before the Lord (Lev. 10:1-2).

Does the same God still punish? If so, I deserve to be struck down. Or I know where He could send some lightening bolts—just warn me in time to get out of the way!

God no longer sends down lightening bolts. Nevertheless, there are merits to the teaching that emphasizes a fear of God's wrath and punishment when we disobey Him. The purpose of punishment from disobedience was to highlight the ugliness of sin and how sin separates us from God. **Thankfully, God did not send His Son to condemn the world, but rather to save it, through belief in His Son, and a life of obedience, starting with repentance, confession, and baptism** (John 3:16-18, 14:23, Acts 2:38, Rom. 10:9-13).

Considering the confusion surrounding God's forms of punishment and whether or not we are subject to them once we are in Christ, here are some questions we will answer in this chapter, inviting God to have the last word through the truth of His Word:

> ➢ Can God's forgiveness pardon my punishment?

> ➢ Will God's grace cleanse the guilt and shame of my bad decisions?

> ➢ Does God's redemption erase the consequences of my sin?

Before we continue, allow me to clarify that the original purpose of the Law and of the consequences of sin was to

remind us of God's holiness and draw us back to Him through repentance and obedience.

 What confusion have you heard about or experienced regarding God's punishment and the consequences of our sin?

Painful Punishment for My Past... Or So I Thought: Maryellen's Story

After becoming a Christian, Maryellen fought the direct lie that God was punishing her for her past. Let's hear her story in her own words.

I grew up in a very dysfunctional family with an alcoholic father and very controlling mother. I entered into a cycle of behavior in my teens of trying to find love through guys. I allowed them to coerce me into physical relationships because I thought that was their way of showing me that they loved me. Little did I know at that time that there is only one perfect love—Our Heavenly Father.

I was faithful to each man when I was with him, but I had one boyfriend who was not faithful to me. I found that out when I went for my annual exam. I had contracted a sexually transmitted disease. Fortunately, it was curable.

After that happened, I moved away and lived with some family members, which was when I found Christ. I became a Christian when I was 23, but my old ways didn't change. I was still trying to find my identity in men, not Christ. I went through Adult Children of Alcoholics (ACOA) therapy and realized my unhealthy pattern.

I met a Christian guy who was very different from all the other men I had dated and a year later we were married. It wasn't until I met him that I ever wanted to have children. My thought was, "I could have children with this man! He would be a great father." I went off birth control and a year later, I still wasn't pregnant. I talked to my doctor about it, and she told me I "needed to relax!"

Another year went by and I still wasn't pregnant. At this point I started to get really frustrated and wondered, "Am I being punished for my past sins? I thought God forgave us and remembered our sins no more?! As far as the east is to the west?! I thought that when I was baptized that ALL my sins were erased?!" And yet another year went by.

My husband got moved into an office with a coworker whose wife had suffered with fertility issues for thirteen years. She saw a doctor in Houston that performed surgery on her and was able to help her conceive. This was after four previous surgeries with other doctors. I believe that God put this man in my husband's office to lead us to this doctor.

We didn't live in Houston, so we had to travel back and forth in order to see him. I had surgery and it seemed successful in giving us hope. I decided I needed to find a local doctor to continue with the process.

At this point I was still very discouraged, but God gave me hope one Sunday. While I was taking communion, I flipped in my Bible to Isaiah 54:1. "Sing, O barren woman, you who never bore a child; burst into song, shout for joy, you who were never in labor..." I felt that God was speaking directly to me and was going to answer my prayer!

Month after month I waited for God. I really questioned Him and thought maybe I was just imagining that He was going to answer our prayers. Was I being punished for my past sins? Did God really forgive me? It definitely wasn't as long as Sarah had to wait, but six months seems like an eternity when you are trying to get pregnant. It had been almost four and a half years since I had gone off of birth control. I finally gave up that I was ever going to have children. But God's timing is perfect. I got pregnant!

We now have two beautiful children that we are raising in the Lord.

The truths that I came to realize were:

God does not punish us for our sins once we are forgiven, but we do have to suffer the consequences of our actions. *The STD I had contracted probably caused damage to my reproductive organs. God was able to use the doctors that I saw in order to help me get pregnant.*

The sins of my past do not define me. God does.

Christ's blood makes me clean every day.

*The doctors never knew the "official" reason why I couldn't get pregnant. But I do know that **God knew the desires of my heart and had a plan for me.** Jeremiah 29:11.*

Maryellen didn't let Satan or the doctors have the last word. She trusted in the abundant hope that comes only from God, no matter what the result.

*Shadrach, Meshach and Abednego replied to him, "King Nebuchadnezzar, we do not need to defend ourselves before you in this matter. If we are thrown into the blazing furnace, the God we serve is able to deliver us from it, and he will deliver us from Your Majesty's hand. **But even if he does not,** we want you to know, Your Majesty, that we will not serve your gods or worship the image of gold you have set up." (Dan. 3:16-18)*

 What other truth would you like to affirm for Maryellen or for yourself?

Punishment from God, Satan, Self or Others?

Satan wants us to allow punishment or consequences to eternally separate us from God's love—to remain focused on the pain and the sadness. He wants to move us from "you did a bad thing" to "you are a bad person." And he wants to convince us that we should receive continual punishment here on earth for the wrong we have done, even after we have been forgiven and are striving to "walk in the light as [God] is in the light" (1 John 1:7).

Others may try to make me feel guilty or "punish me" for my behavior, but no one can put that guilt on me if I have been freed in Christ. Consequently, the other person may not forgive me, but I can rest in the truth that God has forgiven me and released me from that punishment.

We cannot allow Satan to get what he wants! We have a choice to give God the last word. Remember Peter? He betrayed Jesus, but his sole identity was not that of a betrayer. Understanding the gravity of his sin, he repented, embraced God's forgiveness and became a spokesman for God in the early days of the church (Acts 2, 4:20, 10).

If we give Satan the last word, **another lie that tag-teams behind the one that God is punishing me for my sins is that I must continue to punish myself, even after I have been forgiven.**

Self-punishment takes on various forms, i.e. negative self-talk, or self-harm, like cutting. Self-harm, which can be an indication of guilt or unexpressed pain, has become more common and is a manifestation of emotional pain, the desire for control, or the inability to express negative feelings. These thoughts (lies of Satan) outweigh the belief in forgiveness. **However, the lie of "a** life doomed to pain" can be overcome by the abundance of hope stemming from the truth of God's promises of mercy, forgiveness, and freedom.

Self-mutilation in its physical form (i.e. cutting, burning, drinking harmful substances like bleach) presents itself in more teenagers or young adults, and in more young women than men. Whether you self-harmed as a teen or struggle with some of those same urges now, either physically, mentally, or emotionally, there is hope.

For those of you that are unfamiliar with this scheme of Satan, I would like to share a truth my friend clung to when she was cutting and battled the specific lie: "Even if God has forgiven me, there is no way to forgive myself."

"When I first started cutting and a friend found out, he wrote me a note encouraging me to stop or find help (its been a while since I needed to reference it!) The MOST important part was that he left this verse on it: "But he was pierced for our transgressions, he was crushed for our iniquities" (Isa. 53:5). He reminded me that no matter what guilt or shame or unworthiness that was causing me to hurt myself, that Jesus already hurt for me, that He shed His blood for those sins and that guilt. What a blessing! That really has stuck with me all these years since!"

Guilt is often a major factor in self-harm or self-punishment. And Satan, of course, longs to have the last word and steal our hope.

Guilt, Punishment, and Consequences Redefined

Guilt, punishment, and consequences are intertwined in their meaning, but are three distinct concepts that Satan tries to twist and distort in our understanding, leaving us burdened by the entrapping shadow of his lies.

Conversely, God's truth about these terms allows us to recognize the lie, replace it with truth, and remember the truth, abounding in the hope that Satan tries to steal.

How would you define these concepts?

Guilt

Punishment

Consequence

My summary of the three, with an added explanation of shame, would be as follows:

Guilt is brought on by the individual, but can be forgiven. **Shame** is the feeling that accompanies guilt, real or perceived. It can be influenced by the outside pressure (good or bad) to perform in a certain way or not. God allows us to feel shame in order that we might be led to repentance. But Satan wants us to allow the shame and guilt to define us, forgetting God's invitation to be transformed.

Punishment can be self-inflicted or others-inflicted, as with sentencing after a trial in the judicial system—it is a result of the guilt, but it can also be forgiven. **Consequences** are situation-inflicted and a natural byproduct, which cannot be escaped: cause and effect.

Satan wants to convince us that the consequences that come from our actions or the decisions of others are the same as God punishing us (just as Maryellen shared in her story). That is simply not true. Consequences and punishment are two different things.

God is even able to cleanse our consciences and remove the feeling of shame. He can wash us clean of the guilt and remove the weight of our sin. In Christ, He frees us from the punishment and releases us from its bondage. However, we must still face the natural consequences of our decisions.

 When and how does this forgiveness and cleansing happen? (Don't forget to quote the Bible!)

Guilt, Punishment, and Consequences Illustrated

Allow me an illustration to define the terms before we examine additional Bible verses for clarification on these concepts.

I have two friends, let's call them Sally and Sue. They loved to gossip over a cup of coffee and believed the lie that "It's just words, so it won't hurt anyone." One morning, Sue ran into her neighbor, Joy. And before she could share the latest piece of juicy gossip she had heard from Sally, Joy invited her to a ladies' Bible study in her home.

"No worries," Sue thought, equipped with her morsel of neighborly information to tell. "I'll go and can share it as a prayer request" (another entrapping lie). Sitting across the living room was the object of her nugget of gossip, tearful about her present situation. Sue felt convicted. Before the Bible was opened or prayers were offered, God's truth of the consequences of her gossip were staring her in the face.

After Joy concluded the morning's study, Sue approached her and apologized for words she had spoken in the past about Joy and others. Sue committed, in that moment, to break the cycle of gossip, even if Sally was unwilling.

Sally and Sue's relationship dwindled because of Sue's recognition of the lies she had fallen into, as well as her determination that her relationship with God was more important. Sally found other friends with whom to gossip, and while Sue mourned the loss of that friendship, she was determined to live forgiven and repentant. She even hoped to mend the relationships with previous objects of her gossip.

Using the above scenario…

Who was guilty of the sin?

Who was deserving of the punishment?

Who was freed from the guilt and the punishment because of her repentance and God's grace and forgiveness?

Who was still guilty and will receive the punishment unless someday she comes to Christ, repents, and seeks God's forgiveness?

List all those who suffer any consequences of the sin. (*Notice that sometimes we suffer the consequences of other people's sin, even if we don't share in the guilt or punishment.*)

 When you gather with your Iron Rose Sisters in the small group context, discuss your thoughts about guilt, punishment, and consequences, especially in the context of the illustration about gossip.

Guilt, Punishment, and Consequences in the Bible

These terms are often interchanged and confused in our everyday conversation. Can you see how Satan's lies try to twist and distort the truth of what God teaches? Let's give God the last word and remember the truth!

 What does Exodus 20:4-6 say about guilt, punishment, or consequences?

Now, let's see how God spoke through Ezekiel to clarify the concepts of guilt, punishment, or consequence, especially regarding what the Israelites may have misunderstood from Exodus 20.

Read Ezekiel 18:20-32, in order to fill in the blanks and answer the following questions, based on those verses.

"The one who _____ is the one who _____" (v. 20).

Who is guilty for the father's sin? _____

Who is guilty for the son's sin? _____

Using the same verses in Ezekiel, is sin an immediate and permanent condemnation to death? Why or why not?

What hope or promise does God offer in Ezekiel 18?

What truth do we see in 2 Peter 3:9 that affirms these same concepts?

And what is the promise in Hebrews 9:14 and 10:22?

Once we are in Christ, what happens when we sin again? Are we instantly doomed? How do the following scriptures answer those questions?

Romans 6:1

Romans 8:1

1 John 1:5-10

Bringing the Lies and Sin to Light

Growing up in Louisiana, I am familiar with cockroaches—the very large kind that even fly on occasion. Ugh. It makes my skin crawl to start thinking about them. Stick with me for a second and don't skip to the next section because you are cringing with me.

What makes cockroaches and other bugs flee more quickly than anything? Light! We have compared truth to light a number of times in this book. David pled with God to send His light and truth to lead him (Ps. 43:3). **We cannot leave the entrapping lies of the past nor reclaim hope if we are unwilling to expose them to God's light and truth.**

"Do not expect God to cover what you are not willing to uncover."[18]

Secrets keep us sick. And sin is the worst poison of all.

Satan uses shame to keep things in the dark. Yet when we share truth, even ugly truths about ourselves, Satan loses his power over us. **His lies are exposed and he begins to flee because he cannot handle the light of truth.** God is light. Christ is truth. What hope does Satan have when faced with the presence of God?

Look back at what 1 John 1:9 says about confession.

---

[18] Duncan Campbell, a Scottish preacher

And what does 2 Corinthians 7:9-11 say about the exposure of lies or past sin?

God does not tolerate sin. And He hates lies. What He longs for, instead, is repentance, redemption, and a transformation of life from the entrapping lies to an abundant life of faith, hope, and love as He defines them.

The past is familiar, even if it was miserable. And if we fail to remember God's provision and salvation, our forgetful selves lose perspective when we face a new trouble. We cry out to go back—to return to the slavery of our past, in Egypt, just as the Israelites did in Numbers 14:1-4.

So, let's leave those lies in the past, replace them with truth, and remember the truth through the Lie/Truth Chart, starting on the next page. I have filled in the first three rows based on the stories and verses already shared in this chapter. Please fill in the blanks found in the next two rows (#s 4 & 5) to recognize, replace, or remember in ways specific to your struggles, inspired by what we have discussed in this chapter. A final blank row (#6) is included in order that you can invite God to have the last word in an additional lie you face.

RECOGNIZE the lie (in your own words)	REPLACE the lie with truth (in your own words)	REMEMBER the truth (biblical reference)
1. Maryellen's lie: God is punishing me for my past.	God doesn't punish me for my already forgiven, past sins, but I may have to face some of the conse-quences of my actions. God has a bigger plan for me.	"For I know the plans I have for you," declares the Lord, "plans to prosper you and not to harm you, plans to give you hope and a future." **Jer. 29:11**
2. Sin has such a hold on me that it isn't even worth fighting it anymore.	We can be forgiven, washed clean, redeemed!	"Cleanse me with hyssop, and I will be clean; wash me, and I will be whiter than snow." **Ps. 51:7** "If we confess our sins, he is faithful and just and will for-give us our sins and purify us from all unrighteousness." **1 John 1:9**
3. I am suffering the punishment of my family's bad patterns and I'm doomed to repeat them.	I can break the destructive cycle and find hope in Christ's redemption. I am a new creation, made new and made	Ez. 18:20-32 "I have been crucified with Christ and I no longer live, but Christ lives in me. The life I now live in the body, I live by

	whole in Christ.	faith in the Son of God, who loved me and gave himself for me." Gal. 2:20
RECOGNIZE	**REPLACE**	**REMEMBER**
4. The natural consequences of sin (mine or someone else's) are God's way of punishing me.		
5.		"The Lord is compassionate and gracious, slow to anger, abounding in love. He will not always accuse, nor will he harbor his anger forever; he does not treat us as our sins deserve or repay us according to our iniquities. For as high as the heavens are above the earth, so great is his love for those who fear him; as far as the east is from the west, so far has he removed our transgressions from us." Ps. 103:8-12

RECOGNIZE	REPLACE	REMEMBER
6.		

Our mistakes and our past do not define us. In Christ, we are a new creation, walking in newness of life (Rom. 6:4). The old is gone and the new has come (2 Cor. 5:17). We can know the truth and that truth will set us free (John 8:32)!

As new creations, Peter would rather not be known for his betrayal. Rahab wishes that her fame were more for saving the spies than being a prostitute in her former life. The list continues in Hebrews 11 as we reflect on the examples in the "Faith Chapter." And Paul had such a desire to leave his past behind that he changed his name from Saul.

"Forgetting what is behind and straining toward what is ahead, I press on toward the goal to win the prize for which God has called me heavenward in Christ Jesus" (Phil. 3:13b-14).

May the stories from Scripture and present-day testimonies of Christian sisters serve as **an inspiration and a reminder of the truth that God desires to redeem our past, not punish us for it.** Let's give Him the last word of hope and redemption!

Common Threads

An area in which you'd like to grow or bloom—abounding in faith, hope, and love through truth.

_____

_____

A thorn (lie) you'd like to remove and replace with truth.

_____

_____

An area in which you'd like to dig deeper or need someone to hold you accountable (help to recognize the lie or remember the truth).

_____

_____

A verse or truth to remember that speaks to a lie mentioned in this chapter.

_____

_____

CHAPTER 11

Lie: I am Not Enough

You is kind. You is smart. You is important. – Aibileen Clark, *The Help*[19] movie

Lying to ourselves is more deeply ingrained than lying to others. – Fyodor Dostoyevsky

God does not require that each individual shall have the capacity for everything. – Richard Rothe (German Lutheran theologian)

There is a description of genius credited to Albert Einstein: Ask a fish to climb a tree, or an elephant to scale a mountain and they will feel inadequate, compared to a monkey or a goat.

We are not all gifted with the same talents or abilities, nor are we expected to fill the role that others fill. We easily fall into the trap of comparison, coupled with the lies of unrealistic expectations.

---

[19] DreamWorks, 2011.

"I'm inadequate and the rest of the world is going to figure that out!"

Moses the stutterer, Zaccheus the shorty, David, the youngest, Ehud, the lefty, and Deborah, the woman. Thomas, the doubter, Peter, the betrayer, Elijah, the defeated, Sarah, the barren, and Mary, the young virgin.

None of these individuals felt adequate for the task to which God called them.

Feeling Inadequate to the Task

He wanted to conduct. His conducting style, however, was idiosyncratic. During soft passages, he'd crouch extremely low. For loud sections, he'd often leap into the air, even shouting to the orchestra.

His memory was poor. Once he forgot that he had instructed the orchestra not to repeat a section of music. During the performance, when he went back to repeat that section, they went forward, so he stopped the piece, hollering, "Stop! Wrong! That will not do! Again! Again!"

For his own piano concerto, he tried conducting from the piano. At one point, he jumped from the bench, bumping the candles off the piano. At another concert he knocked over a choirboy.

During one long, delicate passage, he jumped high to cue a loud entrance, but nothing happened because he had lost count and signaled the orchestra too soon.

As his hearing worsened, musicians tried to ignore his conducting and get their cues from the first violinist.

Finally the musicians pled with him to go home and give up conducting, which he did.

He was Ludwig van Beethoven.

As the man whom many consider to be the greatest composer of all time learned, no one is a genius of all trades.[20]

As Each Part Does Its Work

"Now if the foot should say, "Because I am not a hand, I do not belong to the body," it would not for that reason stop being part of the body" (1 Cor. 12:15).

We each have a role and a place in the body. You may feel like you are only the pinky fingernail, but when my ear itches, that is exactly the body part I need! Ask a cancer patient about the importance of nose hair after the chemo has caused her to lose all her hair.

My point? **Every single member of the body is important and every single member of the body has an important role to play.** When we fall into the entrapping lies of comparison, we feel inadequate, insufficient, and worthless.

"As each part does *its* work" (Eph. 4:16, *emphasis added*). Each member is called to do *its* part, not someone else's. The hand can't function as the heart. The kidney can't replace the spleen. And if the ankle were to attempt to be a wrist, we would roll our eyes and shake our heads at the ridiculous nature of that proposition.

---

[20] David Sacks, 1001 Quotes, Illustrations, and Humorous Stories for Preachers, Teachers, and Writers, pg. 268

When I compare my abilities to what God has called someone else to do or to be, I will always fall short (Gal. 6:3-5). God knit each of us together in our mother's womb (Ps. 139:13), and created each one as a uniquely amazing individual.

And even though there are some things that God calls all of us to, like teaching, we don't all do it in the exact same way.

 No matter what we are called to do, how we lead, teach, or follow, what is the purpose of our tasks and our place here on earth? (See 2 Cor. 4:7, Eph. 3:20.)

From Powerless to Power

There comes a point when you let the phrase, "It is finished," come out of you. I have learned what I can learn; I have fought as much as I can fight. I have clung to this lie long enough. I am ready to be free.

But the most difficult moment is when I have to finally say, "It is finished" and fully let the lie go. "¡No más!" (No more!)

Just as Jesus said, "It is finished" and gave up His spirit, it was not the end of the story. In dying to self, the old life is past. **In killing the lie, there is resurrection of a new life to be found!**

My friend Katie tells the story of a time when she was crumbled in a heap in the bathroom floor, days before speaking at a Ladies' Retreat. Feelings of inadequacy flooded her and crippled her. "There was no way that God wanted to use *me* to speak to these ladies!" These and many other lies came cascading in, leaving Katie unable to breathe.

Then, it was moments before the retreat was supposed to start and Katie was to speak. She felt attacked by Satan's lies, verbalized through an offhand comment by someone there, shattering Katie's confidence in what God could do through her.

Claiming a power not her own, Katie said, "Enough! It is finished! Away from me, Satan! If I've been asked to do this, then God will give me the strength and the words to make something good come out of it." She was done with the lies Satan was filling her head with at that time. She leaned on God's strength to sustain her and His Spirit to speak through her.

May you be blessed with the strength to say, "It is finished." Not to give up, but to give it over to God: A transfer from (our) powerlessness to (His) power! **A total rejection of Satan and his lies gives God the last word.**

We are merely clay jars, broken vessels, filled to the brim with God's all-surpassing power (2 Cor. 4:7). And we can remember this truth: "Greater is he that is in me than he that is in the world," (1 John 4:4) when we feel weak and incapable.

 Share a time when God's power was seen through your powerlessness.

Jehovah is Still God

Gladys Aylward, missionary to China more than fifty years ago, was forced to flee when the Japanese invaded Yangcheng. But she could not leave her work behind. With only one assistant, she led more than a hundred orphans over the mountains toward Free China.

During Gladys's harrowing journey out of war-torn Yang-cheng... she grappled with despair as never before. After passing a sleepless night, she faced the morning with no hope of reaching safety. A thirteen-year-old girl in the group reminded her of their much-loved story of Moses and the Israelites crossing the Red Sea.

"But I am not Moses," Gladys cried in desperation.

"Of course you aren't," the girl said, "**but Jehovah is still God!**"

When Gladys and the orphans made it through, they proved once again that no matter how inadequate we feel, God is still God and we can trust Him.[21]

The Times When Moses Felt Adequate and Inadequate

Gladys looked to Moses as the pillar of strength and fearless leader of the Israelites when crossing the Red Sea, yet Moses might not have agreed with her. He felt inadequate to carry God's message of freedom to Pharaoh. "But Moses said to God, 'Who am I, that I should go to Pharaoh and bring the Israelites out of Egypt?'" (Ex. 3:11)

---

[21] *The Hidden Price of Greatness*, by Ray Besson and Ranelda Mack Hunsicker as quoted by Jonathan G. Yandell in Rowell, Edward K., ed., *1001 Quotes, Illustrations, and Humorous Stories for Preachers, Teachers, and Writers* (Grand Rapids: Baker Books, 2008), 277.

Moses said to the Lord, 'O Lord, I have never been eloquent, neither in the past nor since you have spoken to your servant. I am slow of speech and tongue.' The Lord said to him, 'Who gave man his mouth? Who makes him deaf or mute? Who gives him sight or makes him blind? Is it not I, the Lord? Now go; I will help you speak and will teach you what to say.' But Moses said, 'O Lord, please send someone else to do it.' (Ex. 4:10-13)

The ironic thing is that prior to his time in Midian, Moses *did* feel adequate as a speaker and leader. Allow me to share Stephen's account of Moses' life as told from Moses' perspective (Acts 7:17-40).

I was no ordinary child. From an early age, everyone knew I was special. To start with, I was the only kid in my grade—the only Hebrew kid.

My Hebrew roots were obvious because of how I looked, but I was safe in Pharaoh's house, raised by his daughter. God had been merciful.

Even though the king had ordered that all the newborn babies be killed, my mom sent me down the river in a basket and Pharaoh's daughter rescued me. My sister, Miriam, was watching nearby, just as she was always taking care of me. Then, at Miriam's suggestion, mom was able to nurse me and tell me stories of Jehovah God in the Egyptian palace.

The stories of Jehovah God intermingled with the education and wisdom of the Egyptians by whom I was trained.

My life was easy and blessed. I was "powerful in speech and action" (Acts 7:22), but I knew the pain and oppression of my people, the Israelites. So, when I was about forty, I was ready. I had known my whole life that I was saved for a special purpose—to save God's people. And I was ready to step up and fulfill my calling. "I've got this," I thought.

So when I decided to visit my own people, and saw one of them being mistreated by an Egyptian, I went to his defense and killed the Egyptian.

I was sure that by avenging that Israelite, the people would realize that God was using me to rescue them (Acts 7:25). However, that was not how it played out.

The next day, some Israelites were fighting and I tried to step in, but what I had done the day before backfired on me and my leadership was rejected.

Dejected and discouraged, I fled to Midian where I settled as a foreigner, married, and had two sons. I stayed in Midian forty years, mostly working as a shepherd, which gave me a lot of time to reflect on what I had done and how I had mishandled things.

> ➤ *God had a plan for my life, but I had taken it into my own hands and was trying to make it happen in my way and in my timing.*
> ➤ *God didn't use me when I was young, "powerful of speech and action," but rather when I was older, more humble, and stuttered.*
> ➤ *God waited until I let go of trying to control how He saved His people, so that I could be used simply as an instrument in His hands.*

Unfortunately, I always struggled with taking matters back into my own hands, especially when the people grumbled and complained.

And I paid a bitter price for not leaving it in God's hands and not trusting Him and His plan. I struck the rock twice instead of speaking to it (Num. 20:1-14). By taking it in my own hands, I rejected God and was unable to enter the Promised Land.

While I never stepped foot into the promised land of Canaan, God's grace is great and I do, now, taste the profound goodness of God in the eternal Promised Land.

Throughout his life, Moses failed most when he considered himself enough and tried to do things his way instead of God's.

Who is Really Enough?

 Which is the greater lie: I am enough or I am not enough?

 Which lie is more dangerous: I am enough or I am not enough? Why?

Satan uses *both* lies to trap us because they are more focused on self than on God.

U.S. wrestler, Helen Maroulis, won a historic gold medal in the 2016 Summer Olympics. She beat Japanese, Saori Yoshida, who had dominated the sport in her weight category as a three-time Olympic and 13-time world champion. Even though the women were of the same weight, the match was compared to David taking on Goliath, according to the media. In the interview following her dramatic win, Helen was asked how she was able to go up against and defeat such an opponent. "I just kept repeating, 'Christ in me. I am enough. Christ in me. I am enough.'" What a powerful testimony on a world stage of a definitive declaration that gave God the last word!

When the focus is on self, we are never enough. And we fall victim to Satan's lies that hinder us from fulfilling God's call. By relying on self and our inadequacies, we forget that God seeks a spirit willing to let Him prepare and use us (Is. 6:8).

Teaching the Truth from the Heart: Edna's Example

One specific way in which that debilitating and hindering lie plays out is that you must have a Bible degree in order to teach a Bible class.

I know many sisters in Christ who have been beaten down by that lie, even as it was spoken by other members of the church. It is my prayer that we can dispel that lie and, instead, encourage, inspire, equip, and empower each of you in your journey with the Father through the blessing of teaching.

I acknowledge that we all have different spiritual gifts. Ephesians 4 talks about how God created some to be teachers, some to be evangelists, some to be apostles, etc. However, teaching takes on various forms and we are all commanded in Matthew 28:18-20 to make disciples. What are the two vital elements of making disciples, as clarified in that passage?

As I was sharing Satan's lie [not being enough as a teacher] with LaNae, her eyes filled with tears in memory of a dear sister Edna Gorton, with whom she worked in children's Bible classes many years ago. Edna had no formal educational training; she did not have a college degree; she even admitted to feeling intimidated by LaNae's classroom decorations and lesson plans, as LaNae is a formally trained educator. However, **Edna was a dedicated student of the Word and fervent in prayer.** She prepared countless lessons, in her own special way, which touched the lives of each and every child who came through her door.

On one particular occasion, LaNae had the opportunity to sit in on one of Edna's classes—a class on girding up your loins. LaNae, upon retelling me this story, touched with emotion, shared how memorable and clear the lesson was—and not only applicable to children, but for anyone of any age. After that class, LaNae shared with Edna how special her method of teaching was and how clearly she communicated the truths of the Word. "Please don't ever stop teaching in the way that God has equipped you to teach!" she told her.

LaNae continued, to me, "I wonder, to this day, if we could find the number of children she impacted with her teaching and her life. I always think of Edna when I think of someone who doesn't feel properly trained to teach. **Please share with any women you know that formal education had nothing to do with Edna's abilities or heart to lovingly teach the truths of God's Word.**"

Amen! I couldn't agree more and could not have stated more clearly the truth with which God longs to empower each of you.

Training and Inadequacy

Paul, himself said, "I may indeed be untrained as a speaker, but I do have knowledge..." (2 Cor. 11:6). In his previous letter, Paul clarified in greater detail his personal inadequacy and the vital role God's Spirit played in equipping him.

Fill in the following blanks from 1 Corinthians 2:1-5 (NIV):

"When I came to you, I did not come with
_____ as I proclaimed to you
the testimony about God. For I resolved to know nothing while I
was with you except _____
_____. I came to you

_____

_____. My message and my
preaching were not with wise and persuasive words, but with a
demonstration of _____,
so that your faith might not rest on human wisdom, but on God's
power."

Who does Matthew 10:19-20 say will do the speaking?

My friend Katie shares, "It makes me think of Bo Shero, one of
the elders who conducted interviews as we prepared to go onto
the mission field. When Bo noticed that my husband, Jeff, was a
little intimidated by the Bible degrees held by the other men that
were applying for the team, he said, 'Don't ever feel bad because
you don't have a degree. You have a lifetime of being a Christian
and you can teach something to these other guys.' POWERFUL
words from an elder at a critical time! **Words of truth that
empowered my husband, Jeff, to hold on to the Word instead
of a degree in Bible.**"

Who are you giving the last word? And on whose word do you
depend when it is your turn to teach?

Does teaching look the same for everyone? Of course
not! List three different forms of teaching and be sure
that at least one of your examples is a non-traditional
way of teaching.

Fill in the second row of the Lie/Truth Chart below with your own lie and truth about teaching.

RECOGNIZE the lie (in your own words)	REPLACE the lie with truth (in your own words)	REMEMBER the truth (biblical reference)
1. I can't teach that class. I don't know enough.	God can work and speak through anyone who is willing to study, prepare, and be used by Him.	"Here I am! Send me." Is. 6:8
2.		

Satan causes us to question our identity, our abilities, our role, and therefore our worth. He attacked Jesus' identity in the temptation (if You are the Son of God...). And he attacks our identity with the same tenacity.

What or Who Determines Your Worth?

All the ways that I had used previously to define myself had been stripped away. I was no longer a missionary or a minister. I was denied the chance to be a wife and mother. My health hindered me from doing much of what I felt called to do. What was left?

Through weeks of sleepless nights and lengthy prayers, I cried out to God for His guidance. I wanted to know my next steps and what to DO. Because what I did defined me, right? I had allowed my role or my position as a servant of God in His church to determine my place, my worth, my identity, and my value. And I felt that without these things, I wasn't enough. **I had lost sight of the only true identity that mattered.**

Through my wrestling, I came to realize a deeper truth. **I am a daughter of the King. And that is enough.** If I am identified in no other way, my identity as a child of God is enough.

I did not come to make or own that simple statement through a simple or short process. Nevertheless, I love that I can now cling to that truth and remember it when I feel Satan's attacks on my self-worth.

When we remember the truth of who we are and whose we are, we give God the last word. We abound in His love, instead of wallowing in Satan's lies.

What better identity is there than that of the child of the King? You are a princess and an heir to the throne (1 John 3:1)!

According to Scripture, what other promises or descriptions does God use for our identity that can we remember and cling to?

Who's Your Daddy?

Joseph's brothers thought they would be happier and that their dad would pay them more attention if they got rid of their younger brother, daddy's favorite. However, after throwing Joseph in a pit and later selling him into slavery, the brothers lived in torment, not happiness, until Joseph reassured them and spoke kindly to them. "Don't be afraid. Am I in the place of God? You intended to harm me, but God intended it for good to accomplish what is now being done, the saving of many lives" (Gen. 50:19-20).

Joseph's brothers were jealous of his happiness and the relationship he had with his father, but **the defining relationship in Joseph's life was not with his father Jacob, but rather with his Father God.**

The father of lies has no place, but his lies of jealousy are entrapping and throw us into a deeper pit than Joseph's brothers threw him. Jealousy and comparison are tandem traps that dig us deeper into the lies.

"We often struggle with insecurity because we compare our behind the scenes with everyone else's highlight reel."[22] Facebook makes this a harsher reality. The pictures and stories shared are filtered to show only the prim, proper, and polished version of our lives. I don't know about you, but my "everyday" pales in comparison to others' vacations, their Pinterest-level perfection projects, the witty quotes, and cute pictures.

[22] Anonymous

Which of the following statements have you most identified with (now or in the past)?

I am not <u>strong</u> enough.

I am not <u>beautiful</u> enough.

I am not <u>smart</u> enough.

I am not <u>loved</u> enough.

I am not <u>popular</u> enough.

I am not <u>good</u> enough.

I am not _____ enough.

 How does our perspective change after reading the following verses?

1 John 3:1-3

Romans 5:6-8

Philippians 3:7-14

Using one of the "not enough" statements above, fill in the Lie/Truth Chart on the next page. Be sure to select the statement with which you most identify, and include the biblical reference for the truth you will remember, whether one of the aforementioned verses or another verse of truth.

RECOGNIZE the lie (in your own words)	REPLACE the lie with truth (in your own words)	REMEMBER the truth (biblical reference)

As a way of giving God the last word, write out how you think He would respond to the statement of you feeling like you are "not enough." **Remember God loves you as His daughter, His heir, His princess.**

The Common Threads this week will likely come from the all-sufficiency found in Christ versus our inadequacies. When Paul was faced with his weaknesses, he shared God's last word with us in 2 Corinthians 12. We will close with those words from Paul as a reminder of God's abounding love and grace—the last word and the answer to Satan's lies that attack our shortcomings and insecurities.

*Therefore, in order to keep me from becoming conceited, I was given a thorn in my flesh, a messenger of Satan, to torment me. Three times I pleaded with the Lord to take it away from me. **But he said to me,***

"My grace is sufficient for you, for my power is made perfect in weakness." *Therefore I will boast all the more gladly about my weaknesses, so that Christ's power may rest on me. That is why, for Christ's sake, I delight in weaknesses, in insults, in hardships, in persecutions, in difficulties. For when I am weak, then I am strong.* (2 Cor. 12:7b-10)

Common Threads

 An area in which you'd like to grow or bloom—abounding in faith, hope, and love through truth.

_____

_____

 A thorn (lie) you'd like to remove and replace with truth.

_____

_____

An area in which you'd like to dig deeper or need someone to hold you accountable (help to recognize the lie or remember the truth).

_____

_____

A verse or truth to remember that speaks to a lie mentioned in this chapter.

_____

_____

CHAPTER 12

Sexual Lies

The Christian ideal has not been tried and found wanting. It has been found difficult and left untried. – G. K. Chesterton

You mustn't force sex to do the work of love, or love to do the work of sex. – Mary McCarthy

Christianity is a demanding and serious religion. When it is delivered as easy and amusing, it is another kind of religion altogether. – Neil Postman

Sex, drugs, and rock 'n roll: the three cardinal sins of the 1980s and early 90s that filtered into every talk given by youth ministers, parents, and others. We were warned about their evil nature, their subliminal messages in music videos (when MTV™ actually showed music videos), and their slippery slopes into unforgivable sins.

Gone were the conversations that elevated sex as a God-given blessing in the context of marriage. "Sex is bad," was the much stronger statement echoed from pulpits, youth rooms, and kitchen tables.

"Sex is like a fire. In a fireplace, it's warm and delightful. Outside the hearth, it's destructive and uncontrollable."[23]

The truths and the lies of a sexual nature are extremely sensitive subjects and can evoke a myriad of emotional and spiritual reactions. As with each of the chapters, I encourage you to enter into this one with lots of prayer, an open mind, and an understanding spirit toward the struggles of others. It is not my intention to offend or to chastise, but rather to give God the last word on this issue—not your words, or mine.

During the same time as "sex, drugs, and rock 'n roll" talks, I clearly remember a young lady at my middle school making a statement in defense of sex with multiple partners. She declared, "It's not like the Bible says anything against it."

My jaw dropped in shock and then set in defiance of the lie she had just pronounced. However, my culture-shocked middle-school self was nearly speechless. I vaguely remember mumbling, "Have you *read* the Bible?" To which she replied, "Well, yeah. And there's nothing in there about it being bad. I mean God created sex."

I do not remember the girl's name, although I do have a vague recollection of her face. I have prayed for her every time I remember that conversation, and think of all the things I wished I had said. I would love to sit down with her and help her recognize the sexual lies, replace them with truth, and remember the truth—all through Scripture.

---

[23] Green, Michael P., ed., *1500 Illustrations for Biblical Teaching* (Grand Rapids: Baker Books, 2005), 333.

In the meantime, back in the late 80's, my conversation with that girl seemed to provide justification to those who were preaching a constant message of, "Sex is bad." These issues were addressed as if they were a new temptation, a new trap by Satan—set and baited with the choicest of cheeses. However, sexual temptations are anything but new.

> ➤ To "corinthianize" meant to practice sexual immorality. It was a Greek word inspired by the city of Corinth, a sex-saturated culture in the days of the early church. Aphrodite's temple was in Corinth and prostitution was practiced in the name of religion.
> ➤ David justified his actions with Bathsheba and the killing of Uriah because of his sexual desire. It took Nathan confronting him directly to realize the sexual lies in which he had entrapped himself (2 Sam. 11-12).
> ➤ We don't get halfway through the book of Genesis before God is ready to destroy entire cities because of their sexual deviancy and rampant sexual behavior in total disregard of God's teaching (Sodom and Gomorrah in Gen. 18-19).

It's safe to say that Satan has been filling our minds with lies regarding sex since the beginning of time. Of course, the father of lies and master deceiver would take one of God's most pleasure-filled creations and distort the truths protecting our sexual design in order that we might fall into the entrapping web of lies surrounding it.

Genesis 2:24 says, "For this reason, a man will leave his father and mother and be united to his wife, and they will become one flesh." One flesh. Union in heart, mind, body, and soul.

When we create union in one of those contexts without the full commitment of the package deal, or alter God's design in any way, we are distorting what God originally intended.

C.S. Lewis put it this way:

The Christian idea of marriage is based on Christ's words that a man and wife are to be regarded as a single organism—for that is what the words 'one flesh' would be in modern English. And the Christians believe that when He said this He was not expressing a sentiment but stating a fact—just as one is stating a fact when one says that a lock and its key are one mechanism, or that a violin and a bow are one musical instrument. The inventor of the human machine was telling us that its two halves, the male and the female, were made to be combined together in pairs, not simply on the sexual level, but totally combined. The monstrosity of sexual intercourse outside marriage is that those who indulge in it are trying to isolate one kind of union (the sexual) from all the other kinds of union, which were intended to go along with it and make up the total union. The Christian attitude does not mean that there is anything wrong about sexual pleasure, any more than about the pleasure of eating. It means that you must not isolate that pleasure and try to get it by itself, any more than you ought to try to get the pleasures of taste without swallowing and digesting, by chewing things and spitting them out again.[24]

God Redeems Negative Sexual Experiences

Do you remember your first crush? Take a moment to remember his name—what he looked like standing across the playground at recess in elementary school. Will you ever forget him?

Now think about your first kiss. His name, where you were, the feelings that were stirred deep inside, the awkwardness of the

---

[24] Lewis, C. S. *Mere Christianity* (New York: Harper Collins, 2001) 104-5.

moment, and maybe even the outfit you were wearing… They are permanently etched in your brain. Are they not?

Would our first sexual experience be any different?

I apologize to those of you for whom your first sexual experience was not what you desired. That is not what God designed and He did not want that for you. I am so sorry that someone took advantage of you because of his/her own selfish, sexual desires. Childhood sexual abuse and rape are not to be taken lightly and I pray that you have come to know God's redeeming power and cleansing in your life. Only God knows the depth of your scars, but I pray you have tasted of the new life that He offers. I am sorry if this chapter is difficult for you, but I pray that you give God the last word in your life.

Satan's lies about sexual abuse are rampant. Allow me to speak words of truth over you: You did not deserve what happened to you. It is not your fault. You *can* be made new. Yes, what happened is a part of your life, but it does not define you. There *are* men who can look past your brokenness and love you for who you are. Not every man (or woman) will treat you that way. God can be trusted. There are trustworthy Christian sisters and counselors in whom you can confide to take steps toward healing. You are not the only one who has gone through this. You are worthy of God's love. You are beautiful.

Before proceeding, take some space below to write out two of the promises from the proceeding paragraph, replacing "you" with "I," and inserting your name.

Example: *I, Michelle, am worthy of God's love.*

Why is Sex Such a Big Deal?

As you are fully aware, many do not follow God's design for love and marriage. And you may have noticed how many of the testimonies shared in this book (and a few others still to come) include falling into a sexual trap as a result of believing other lies. Satan is ruthless in his attacks and works his wiles, sneaks in, and leads us into the temptation.

What is the most intense or dangerous element of sexual sin, as seen in 1 Corinthians 6:18?

 Why is it such a big deal that sexual sins are "against our own body?" What does that mean?

 Does the world agree with the statement that sexual sins are against our own body? How *does* the world describe sexual sin?

Lies About Love

Another way of looking at lies is to compare what the world says with what the Word says (John 17:12, 14-15). Sound familiar? It's just like recognizing the lie and remembering the truth!

 How does 1 John 4:5-6 say that we can clearly recognize the Spirit of truth and the spirit of falsehood?

James also warns us to have our mind and heart crafted by the Word and not the world (James 3:13-18). James and John's parallel warnings highlight the contrast between the Word-view and the worldview. **When we depend on the world's distorted view of love, our view of sex will also be affected.** So, let's clear it up and remind ourselves of God's truth.

What is love?

> ➤ Physical affection or a heart, soul, mind, and strength commitment?
> ➤ Emoticon hearts or loving with all your heart?
> ➤ Self-seeking or seeking to bless and honor others?

 How does the world define love?

Remember, if we know the truth, it will be much easier to recognize the lie.

 What is God's design for sex, love, and marriage? And where do we see that design or definition referenced in the Bible?

Not only does God love us, but He IS love (1 John 4:8). And His love for us is sacrificial (John 3:16), redemptive (Hos. 3:1), and undeserved (Ps. 103:10).

Beloved like a Bride

There is no greater identity than as the bride of Christ (2 Cor. 11:2, Rev. 19:7, 21:9). This promise is for the married and unmarried, single and divorced—whether you have been a bride or have always dreamed of being one.

When I attend a wedding, do you want to guess what my favorite part is? Nope. I can't eat the cake. And the dress, as beautiful as it might be, is not what I look at. My favorite moment in the wedding is when the bride enters and I see the look on the groom's face. Even the most "macho" guys melt. The look of love, longing, pride, and joy is indescribable. His expression mirrors the thought of deep blessing and honor, even surprise at the reality that "She's mine!"

Christ looks at you with the same love, longing, pride, and joy when He sees you as His bride. When we become one with Him in baptism, He is filled with the same sense of blessing and honor that He now gets to call us His. "She's mine!" He declares in excitement and celebration of His beloved.

There is no greater blessing than our identity as the bride of Christ—the culmination of God's many expressions of love throughout all of Scripture.

 What does it mean to be the bride of Christ (the blessings, the responsibilities, and the implications)?

Why would God use the analogy of the bride of Christ for us, as individuals and as a church? (Refer to 2 Cor. 11:2, Rev. 19:7, 21:9, and the surrounding verses.)

God loves you as His treasured and beloved bride!

Small Attacks Become Big Cracks

Satan will do all he can to undermine our identity as the bride of Christ. And he does it in subtle and slow ways...

Scientists now say that a series of slits, not a giant gash, sank the *Titanic*.

The opulent, 900-foot cruise ship sank in 1912 on its first voyage from England to New York. Fifteen hundred people died in the worst maritime disaster of the time.

The most widely held theory is that the ship hit an iceberg, which opened a huge gash in the side of the liner. But an international team of divers and scientists used sound waves to probe through the wreckage, buried in mud two-and-a-half miles deep. Their discovery? The damage was surprisingly small. Instead of the huge gash, they found six relatively narrow slits across the six watertight holds.

Small damage, below the waterline and invisible to most, can sink a huge ship. In the same way, small compromises, unseen to others, can ultimately sink a person's character.[25]

Why So Many Sexual Lies?

When it comes to sexual lies, Satan's influence is extensive. He whittles away at our conviction, just like the cracks in the *Titanic*. And even though the cracks start small, the breadth and depth of his attacks in the sexual context are more prevalent than in any other area. Because of that, I will ask you to forgive this lengthy Lie/Truth Chart. There will be some follow-up questions at the end of the Chart.

RECOGNIZE the lie (in your own words)	REPLACE the lie with truth (in your own words)	REMEMBER the truth (biblical reference)
1. Sex is bad.	God created sex as a beautiful and wonderful thing between a	Song of Solomon[26]

---

[25] Rowell, Edward, ed. *1001 Quotes, Illustrations, and Humorous Stories* (Grand Rapids: Baker Books, 2008), 228-9.

[26] Song of Solomon would not be the most quoted book of the Bible. Some biblical scholars describe it as an allegory for God's love for the church, but the language more clearly mirrors a vivid and intimate relationship between a man and his wife in the privacy of the marriage bed. Many sections of the book cannot be read without blushing. The imagery is poetic and romantic. And, most importantly, it is a reflection of the beauty with which God designed sexual union and delight in marriage.

RECOGNIZE	REPLACE	REMEMBER
	man and a woman, sacred to marriage.	
2. My sexual identity is what defines me.	My identity in Christ is what defines me.	If you are in Christ, you are a new creation. **2 Cor. 5:17**
3. It feels right, so it can't be wrong.	Feelings cannot be trusted.	"The heart is deceitful above all things and beyond cure. Who can understand it?" **Jer. 17:9**
4. Pornography is only an issue for men.	There is a growing trend of female porn addicts.[27]	"Have nothing to do with the fruitless deeds of darkness, but rather expose them. It is shameful even to mention what the disobedient do in secret. But everything exposed by the light becomes visible—and everything that is illuminated becomes a

[27] "In their 2013 Annual Report, Covenant Eyes, an Internet and accountability filtering site, finds that 20 percent of Christian women say they are porn addicts. Among college-age women, 18 percent report spending time online weekly for Internet sex.

XXXchurch, an online Christian resource for porn addicts, cites that 1 in 3 visitors to adult sites are women, 9.4 million women view porn monthly, and 13 percent of women admit accessing porn at work." Maria Cowell. "Porn: Women Use It Too," *Today's Christian Woman* online, February 2015

		light." **Eph. 5:11-13**
RECOGNIZE	**REPLACE**	**REMEMBER**
5. I'm a strong Christian girl. I can put myself in compromising situations or experiment sexually and not be tempted.	Flee does not mean free to get as close as I can without crossing the line.	"Flee from sexual immorality…" **1 Cor. 6:18a** "Do not arouse or awaken love before it so desires." **Song. 2:7, 3:5, 8:4**
6. I've already fallen into the sex trap. I might as well keep having sex since I've already tainted that part of me and I can't get my virginity back.	My body is a temple to be honored. God specializes in redemption. He buys us back with an everlasting love and restores us.	"Do you not know that your bodies are temples of the Holy Spirit, who is in you, whom you have received from God? You are not your own; you were bought at a price. Therefore honor God with your bodies." **1 Cor. 6:19-20**
7. If I wrestle with desires for a same-sex relationship, I am already condemned.	God does not condemn us for our struggles because they are a testimony that we long to avoid giving into the sin.[28]	"For in my inner being I delight in God's law; but I see another law at work in me, waging war against the law of my mind and making me a prisoner of the law of

---

[28] Resource for same-sex attraction struggles, www.centerpeace.org

		sin at work within me. Therefore, there is now no condemnation for those who are in Christ Jesus, because through Christ Jesus the law of the Spirit who gives life has set you free from the law of sin and death." **Rom. 7:22-23, 8:1-2**
RECOGNIZE	**REPLACE**	**REMEMBER**
8. God's definition of marriage has no place in the world today.	God's design for marriage is the answer to many of the world's problems.	"Follow God's example, therefore, as dearly loved children and walk in the way of love, just as Christ loved us and gave himself up for us as a fragrant offering and sacrifice to God. But among you there must not be even a hint of sexual immorality, or of any kind of impurity, or of greed, because these are improper for God's holy people." Eph. 5:1-3

RECOGNIZE	REPLACE	REMEMBER
9. I can flirt with my coworker and not be unfaithful to my husband. He knows I'm a married woman.	Faithfulness to God and to my husband should be a higher priority than a fleeting compliment or flirt.	"As obedient children, do not conform to the evil desires you had when you lived in ignorance. But just as he who called you is holy, so be holy in all you do; for it is written: "Be holy, because I am holy.""' 1 Peter 1:14-15
10. God put this wonderful man in my life.	Just in case you're confused, God will never send you someone else's husband.	"Keep the marriage bed pure." Heb. 13:4
11.		
12.		

Which of the lies or truths jumped out at you from the Lie/Truth Chart above? Why that one?

Before moving on, please add a couple of Lies and Truths to this Chart in numbers 11 and 12. (Don't forget to *Remember the Truth* through a specific scripture.)

How Satan Used Lies in Libby's and Linda's Lives

I want to share two women's stories and thank them for their willingness to share openly how Satan worked in their lives to entrap them with multiple lies, which led them into sexual sin. Their prayer is that you will find hope through their stories and know that you are not alone in your struggles. Even if these have not been your personal struggles, may these stories help you understand more about the lies with which others have struggled.

Libby's Story (continued in Appendix D)

*If a spider's web were one straight line, very few insects would fall prey and be devoured by the spider. While God draws clear lines about sin and abundant life through his word, **Satan weaves a web of lies, making it easier for us to fall into the "grey" areas.** Sometimes that web spans large amounts of time, growing ever wider with each new lie, ever increasing the chances that God's children will unexpectedly find themselves struggling in the sticky trap, as Satan creeps up to devour us. **Satan pursued me for many years, weaving a special web of lies for me that tore down my self worth.***

*Up until I graduated college, my life was headed in the "right" direction. I worked hard at the university, happily walked across the arena floor to accept my diploma, and shortly thereafter boarded a plane to Honduras as I had the previous summers of my college career. I was the mission-minded, servant-hearted, church-going gal. That is not to say that I was without sin. On the contrary, I struggled with sin; but I never felt that Satan had a life-altering hold on my heart. Looking back, **I see that Satan slowly reeled me in—inch by inch, relationship by relationship, he tugged on me. Before I knew it, I didn't even recognize myself.***

*Just before graduating and moving to Honduras (until the political instability sent me home), I met a man who took an interest in me. I was excited because that didn't happen often. In high school, I didn't date. No one pursued me—which really got me **feeling like I was undesirable. Sometimes I let that thought consume me, and Satan started planting seeds of doubt about my value and worth.** I didn't realize how my thoughts about myself were changing at first, until I found myself in a relationship. **Lie #1: My worth and value comes from men.***

[Please see Appendix D, pg. 271 for the rest of Libby's powerful story, which includes the following lies with which Libby wrestled, and truths that set her free.]

Lie: No man will take pride in having me by his side.

Lie: It is okay to be in a relationship with someone who does not share my faith and convictions.

Lie: Sex will save my relationship.

Lie: Because I got myself into this mess, I had to get myself out.

*Truth: **God is bigger.***

*Truth: **I can stand with confidence again knowing my worth as a child of God, not a girlfriend of man.***

Linda's Story

The enemy is so deceiving. He is aware of our weakness and ready to charge when the gates are open. "Your enemy the devil prowls around like a roaring lion looking for someone to devour" (1 Pet. 5:8). **God has entrusted in us to keep Him as our gatekeeper.**

When I thought my gate was secure, I had myself in a very vulnerable position. There is most likely one main reason why I was so vulnerable: I wasn't allowing God to be Lord of my life.

My husband and I had been raising three beautiful children. Dan worked hard to provide, so that I could be a stay at home mom: a privilege I dreamed of being. We were trying our best to raise our children up in the Lord, attending church, making sure they were in Sunday school, involved in youth activities, paying for them to attend a private Christian school, active in our service for God, and surrounded by Christian friends.

We had learned the "way of the Christian life." It was challenging. We had both been raised in loving homes but did not have the example of what a Christian home looked like. I am very grateful for these privileges God granted and blessed us with. And the mercy He had on our parenting skills.

From the outside, our lives looked pretty well intact. **But I had learned to act the part.** *In other words, I was not in a deep enough relationship with God to know Him very well, and to rely on Him, rather than on myself. So one of the first lies I believed that my life was "good enough." Especially when I compared it to my parents', I was doing so much better than what I had been taught. Oh, the sin of arrogance.*

My husband had been running his own business for several years. Being self-employed has many of its own challenges, and it definitely takes much of your time and energy. So, to make this long story short, and so that I don't write my own book within Michelle's book, I will just put this right out there: I fell into the sinful relationship of an affair.

It was a very selfish choice on my part and there are no good excuses. I blame no one but myself. But on the other hand and brighter side of this story, **I have repented, been forgiven and redeemed by the love, grace, and mercy of our amazing and victorious God.** *My husband and family have also granted me that same love and forgiveness. Our marriage is restored! All glory and honor to God!!!!*

It was shortly before my oldest graduated from high school. My kids were becoming more independent, and I wasn't feeling as needed by them. My husband was working very hard to provide and manage his business, so I started feeling lonely and believing many lies:

- ➢ *Lie: I'm not important to my husband.*
- ➢ *Lie: I'm not a priority.*
- ➢ *Lie: I feel so empty.*
- ➢ *Lie: My husband doesn't care about what I'm doing each day.*
- ➢ *Lie: All he wants from me is sex.*
- ➢ *Lie: I deserve better.*
- ➢ *Lie: This other man has become a better friend than my own husband; he cares more about me.*
- ➢ *Lie: This other man knows me and understands me better than even my own family does.*
- ➢ *Lie: God must have brought us together.*

I truly believe if I had been into God's Word and seeking Him for fulfillment, I would not have fallen. *His word is truth and it has the capability to empower, strengthen, protect, and change. And without it, I would have no hope. If I had continued down that road of sin, I would not have the power of God within me to see the truth of His promises now. He brings goodness, mercy, grace, and faithfulness.*

I am forever grateful for God's loving compassion, and His patience. He says He will never leave us. That is a promise, and I believe it! Although I had turned from Him, God still pursued me and fought for me. He loves each and every one of us that much! I praise God for the truth of His Word that brought me out of a slimy pit and back into His loving arms. Even after heading down the road of repentance, I still had to battle with the lies.

> ➢ *Lie: I hurt too many people to be forgiven.*
> ➢ *Lie: My sin is too big to recover from.*
> ➢ *Lie: Even if God forgives me, no one else will.*
> ➢ *Lie: I was so foolish. I should've known better. How could I have done this to my family? (Forgiving myself was a huge battle.)*

*With the support and patience of my loving husband and family, as well as other people in my life that had my best interest at heart, they constantly pointed the way to God. **My willingness and desire to surrender my heart back to God allowed Him to speak truth back into me.** Just a few of the verses, marked in my Bible, which spoke truth, hope, and love over me were these:*

> ➢ *The truth is, God means what He says. "Every word of God is flawless" (Prov. 30:5).*
> ➢ *The truth is, nothing I do or don't do can change the love my God has for me. "For it is by grace you have been saved, through faith, and this is not from yourselves, it is the GIFT of God, not by works, so that no one can boast" (Eph. 2:8-9).*
> ➢ *Truth: I don't have to rely on my own strength. "My grace is sufficient for you, for my power is made perfect in weakness" (2 Cor. 12:9).*
> ➢ *Another truth: God understands me and loves me, a lot! "But you, Lord, are a compassionate and gracious God, slow to anger, abounding in love and faithfulness" (Ps. 86:15).*
> ➢ *Truth: There is hope when I submit to God, and He will restore what I've messed up. "... in all your ways submit to him, and he will make your paths straight" (Prov. 3:6).*
> ➢ *Truth: God wants to protect me and bless my life. "The thief's purpose is to steal and kill and destroy. My purpose is to give life in all its fullness" (John 10:10).*

> *The truth: God knows I will fall and He promises to catch me. "The Lord is trustworthy in all he promises and faithful in all he does. The Lord upholds all who fall" (Ps. 145:13-14).*

Praise God for His most perfect gift, the Bible! There is no other avenue more convicting and empowering than God's Word.

Justification or Repentance?

Do you see the way God guided these women to recognize, replace, and remember? Satan won a few battles, but they each gave God the last word in their lives and claimed victory in His name.

Yet, if we are not careful, we can confuse God's words with Satan's—the wolf in sheep's clothing. Just like Linda did in her lie about the man that was not her husband (also Lie #10 in the Lie/Truth Chart), **we attempt to insert God's name into the lie in order to justify our actions.** What a conniving tactic of Satan! But let's recognize it for the lie that it is and remember the truth of who God is and what He commands.

Because once we have fallen into sin, we grasp at other lies in order to justify our actions. King David did the same thing (2 Sam. 11). Thankfully, that is not where the story ends.

God's Word, through the prophet Nathan, forced David to **recognize** the lies in which he was entrapped and the gravity of his sin (2 Sam. 12). Through his request that God cleanse, renew, and restore him (Ps. 51), he **replaced** these lies with truth.

Linda, Libby, and many of us identify with David's prayer in Psalm 51. He had lost sight of the "joy of his salvation" and this repentant psalm was his cry out to God for forgiveness and redemption.

Can you believe that the man after God's own heart also fell into sexual sin? He certainly did. Yet he **remembered** "God's mercy, unfailing love, and great compassion" after he admitted his sin.

And David came to rest in the truth and the love of God—not the instant gratification of false sexual love with Bathsheba, but rather the unconditional, unfailing, true love of the Father who forgave him.

Which will you choose: the lie of temporary gratification or the truth of eternal sanctification?

Cleanse me with hyssop, and I will be clean;

wash me, and I will be whiter than snow.

Create in me a pure heart, O God,

and renew a steadfast spirit within me. (Ps. 51:7, 10)

Common Threads

 An area in which you'd like to grow or bloom—abounding in faith, hope, and love through truth.

_____

_____

A thorn (lie) you'd like to remove and replace with truth.

_____

_____

An area in which you'd like to dig deeper or need someone to hold you accountable (help to recognize the lie or remember the truth).

_____

_____

A verse or truth to remember that speaks to a lie mentioned in this chapter.

_____

_____

CHAPTER 13

Lie: Grace Means I Have to be Tolerant

God loves us the way we are, but he loves us too much to leave us that way. – Leighton Ford

We pardon in the degree we love. – Francois de la Rochefoucauld

Our culture has accepted two huge lies. The first is that if you disagree with someone's lifestyle, you must fear or hate them. The second is that to love someone means you agree with everything they believe or do. Both are nonsense. You don't have to compromise convictions to be compassionate. – Phil Robertson, Duck Commander

Truth is uncompromising, and so is grace. There is **enough grace** for the self-harming teen, the screaming mom, the strung-out college student, and the addicted sister. There is **grace upon grace** for the 80-year-old with regrets and the impatient three-year-old. **Matchless grace** for the messy house, the imperfect lawn, the frustrating husband, the stained carpet and the tattered heart. **Unmerited grace** for the

236 • MICHELLE J. GOFF

broken marriage, the demanding boss, the unreasonable professor, and the angry driver.

We all long for that kind of uncompromising grace—whether for ourselves or for a loved one.

Truth is no respecter of persons. And neither is grace. The truth about grace, however, may surprise you. **Because the ugly truth of sin is what makes the truth of grace beautiful.** You can't have one without the other.

In addressing the Lie: Grace Means I Have to Be Tolerant, it is important that we understand the meaning of the words grace and tolerance, as God would define them, not as Satan's lies have distorted them.

Dietrich Bonhoeffer refers to it as costly grace in *The Cost of Discipleship.*

> *[Grace] is costly because it costs a man his life, and it is grace because it gives a man the only true life. It is costly because it condemns sin, and grace because it justifies [makes right with God] the sinner. Above all, it is costly because it cost God the life of his Son: 'Ye were bought at a price', and what has cost God much cannot be cheap for us. Above all, it is grace because God did not reckon his Son too dear a price to pay for our life, but delivered him up for us. Costly grace is the Incarnation of God.*[29]

How does God define grace (Rom. 3:20-24, 6:1, 14, 11:6; Eph. 2:8-9; Heb. 4:16)?

---

[29] Bonhoeffer, Dietrich, *The Cost of Discipleship* (New York: Simon and Schuster, 1959), 45.

What is the purpose of grace (ex. Acts 11:19-23, and the above verses)?

But, how does the concept of tolerance enter into God's definition of grace? **The word tolerance has become a popular word, especially in promotion of an attitude that supports relative truth.** The lie: "Whatever works for you is good for you," has taken over as a distorted definition of grace. And absolute truth has been rejected in favor of absolute tolerance.

The following are three ways of looking at the concept of tolerance:

➤ I tolerate my neighbor's dog.
➤ Turn the other cheek (Matt. 5:39).
➤ Don't tolerate sin.

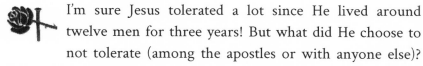 I'm sure Jesus tolerated a lot since He lived around twelve men for three years! But what did He choose to not tolerate (among the apostles or with anyone else)? *Mention specific Bible stories or groups of people with their respective biblical reference.*

Balancing Grace and Truth

Jesus came full of grace **and** truth (John 1:14). He did not compromise the truth when He extended grace. For Him, it was not one or the other; it was always both. He met people where they were and pointed them to the Father—the author of grace and truth.

We cannot extend grace at the expense of truth, nor can we promote truth at the expense of grace.

Grace has been a challenging and confusing concept since the Jews and Gentiles debated its merits. This was one of the primary focuses of the book of Romans. At first glance, throughout the book, it appears that Paul vacillates between the arguments in favor of the Jewish perspective of the Law and then the Gentile's appreciation of grace, but what he highlights is a balance between law and grace. Neither extreme is healthy or what God has designed.

Like Jesus, we have no greater permission to force-feed truth than we do to water down or withhold grace.

For an example of how Jesus put into action true grace, balanced with truth, let's look at the story of the woman caught in the act of adultery (John 8:1-11).

 Who do you most identify with in the story? (Don't limit yourself to thinking only of the sin of adultery—this story applies to any sin or entrapping lie.)

Why did the older men start dropping their stones first?

 What were Jesus' final words to the woman?

Grace AND Truth

The emphasis in the story of the woman caught in adultery is on grace, but not at the expense of truth. What a difficult line to walk—a challenging balance to strike! Do we ever accomplish it as perfectly as Christ did? No. But is it worth striving to communicate both grace and truth? Absolutely!

Jesus is the embodiment and fulfillment of grace and truth (John 1:16-17). If we compromise the true meaning of either grace or truth, we are redefining Christ.

Therefore, we must caution ourselves to not restrict nor redefine God's <u>grace</u>. Neither can we restrict or redefine God's <u>truth</u>.

What does it look like to give grace, as God defines it? What biblical references or stories back this up?

Now, what does it look like to communicate truth, as God would have us to? What are the important points to remember when sharing truth, as stated in God's Word? (Don't forget Eph. 4:15 in your list of verses.)

Speaking the Truth in Love and through Love

A friend of mine is far from God. She used to know Him. But she has chosen to walk away from Him and proclaims she wants nothing to do with God or any conversations about Him. It is painful for those of us that know and love her. We long for her to return to a right relationship with our Father. And we know He will welcome her back in the same way He did for the prodigal son in Luke 15. I can't wait for the party in heaven, and here with us, when she repents and returns.

We wait. We pray. We seek openings in which we can continue to plant and water seeds of her faith. And we ask God to put others in her life that will shine the light of truth *and* grace, as we have discussed in this chapter.

While we wait, as another friend said recently, "In reflecting on the most powerful things that remain, found in 1 Corinthians 13 (faith, hope, and love) I realized something: She doesn't want anything to do with my **faith**. My words of **hope** ring empty in her ears. So, I am left with the task of showing her God's **love**."

And this is my prayer: that your love may abound more and more in knowledge and depth of insight, so that you may be able to discern

what is best and may be pure and blameless for the day of Christ,
filled with the fruit of righteousness that comes through Jesus Christ—
to the glory and praise of God. (Phil. 1:9-11)

 What role do faith, hope, and love play in our
relationships with those in need of grace and truth?

We always thank God, the Father of our Lord Jesus Christ, when we
*pray for you, because we have heard of your **faith** in Christ Jesus and*
*of the **love** you have for all God's people—the **faith** and **love** that*
*spring from the **hope** stored up for you in heaven and about which*
*you have already heard in the **true message of the gospel** that has*
come to you. In the same way, the gospel is bearing fruit and growing
throughout the whole world—just as it has been doing among you
*since the day you heard it and truly understood God's **grace**.* (Col.
1:3-6)

Notice the relationship between faith, hope, and love as they
relate to grace and truth in Colossians 1. What truth does Paul
highlight is of utmost importance?

 How would you share the grace and truth of the gospel
message with someone?

The Great Debate Between Grace and Truth

 Which is harder for you to give: grace or truth? Why?

 Which is harder to accept in your own life: grace or truth? Why?

 Do you find it easier to extend grace to others or to yourself? Why?

 Do we have permission to qualify our response—to only extend grace to those who we think deserve it? Or to hide the truth from those we think are unwilling to hear it?

Knowing My Responsibility

I can't make anyone accept truth, nor can I make anyone accept grace.

 What does the story in Ezekiel 33:1-9 tell us about truthful warnings and our responsibility?

Put a check mark by the things that *are* the responsibility of the man on the watchtower. And cross out the things that he is *not* responsible for.

Watch for the enemy

Let others keep watch in his place

Sound the warning

Only warn his friends and family

Make sure the people prepare for battle

Judge or condemn those who do not heed the warning

Rejoice with those who heed the warning

Mourn over those who did not heed the warning

 What other comments or observations can be made about what is and is not the role of the watchman?

Personal Reflection: What about being a watchman in our own lives... Have we fallen into the trap of Satan's lies and become tolerant of our own sin?

A Gracious Example, Rejected and Accepted

When I was in high school, I was not invited to go hang out with many friends. Those that were smoking pot knew I would be a buzz kill. The ones who were shoplifting knew I wouldn't participate. The cheaters hated to see me study after I refused to let them copy my homework. You get the idea...

I was, by no means, a perfect teenager. You can ask my parents about my pride, my sisters about my bossiness, or my friends about the self-righteous attitude I often adopted. (If you're unfamiliar with the attitude, the older brother in Luke 15 demonstrates it adequately.)

Nevertheless, during my final year of middle school, I was shocked when one girl approached me, waiting for the school bus one crisp fall morning. Totally out of the blue, she asked if I would help her stop cursing.

"You don't curse and I want to know how you do it. I keep getting in trouble with my parents because I can't stop <#*?!> mouthing off. See! I just did it talking to you without realizing it."

"Actually, you did realize it," I responded. "You caught yourself just after you said it. We just need to make you aware of it before you say it instead of right afterward and you'll be able to quit."

"It's easier when I'm talking to you because I know you don't curse. It makes me think more about what I'm saying."

For the next several weeks, we decided to sit together on the bus and talk. When she let a curse word slip, even after we got to school, I would say a code word we had agreed on in order to remind her of her commitment to stop.

Shortly after that time, our family moved to another neighborhood. The girl and I no longer rode the bus together, and since we had no classes together, we lost touch.

I would like to think that our code word and our friendship served her well through the years as she battled cursing or other challenges she faced. I know that our friendship served me greatly.

- ➤ I learned that my silent example spoke volumes.
- ➤ I learned that it is okay to ask for help or be of help to someone else.
- ➤ I learned that we all need a friend who encourages us to be the best version of ourselves.
- ➤ And I learned that a judgmental attitude is a deterrent, but open conversation and relationship can make all the difference.

Upon starting my college years and meeting other girls who had similar goals and convictions as I did, I reflected back on my high school years and the lack of invitations to participate with the "cool girls." I had made my peace with it, and with them. Yet, in the process, I realized that my very presence felt like condemnation because of my lack of participation and unspoken disapproval. However, **I realized that what made the greatest impact was when I engaged in relationship.**

How was Jesus' presence inviting without being condoning?

"They don't care how much you know until they know how much you care." This common expression affirms **the importance of relationship when we consider the concepts of grace, truth, tolerance, and intolerance.**

What are some of the lies associated with grace, truth, tolerance, and intolerance? Fill in the blanks in the final Lie/Truth Chart below:

RECOGNIZE the lie (in your own words)	REPLACE the lie with truth (in your own words)	REMEMBER the truth (biblical reference)
1. I have to agree with you on everything to be your friend.		
2. There are degrees of sin.		"For whoever keeps the whole law and yet stumbles at just one point is guilty of breaking all of it." **James 2:10**
3. My friend is a "good person."		"As it is written: "There is no one righteous, not even one; for all have sinned and fall short of the glory of God," **Rom. 3:10, 23**
4. Grace makes everything "gray."		

RECOGNIZE	REPLACE	REMEMBER
5. I can do whatever I want and God's grace will cover me.		"What shall we say, then? Shall we go on sinning so that grace may increase? By no means!" Rom. 6:1-2a
6.	If you water down sin, you water down grace.	
7. I'm responsible for the choices of others.	I can speak the truth in love, but the other person has free will to make his/her own choices.	
8. That person doesn't deserve grace.	I don't deserve grace.	"For it is by grace you have been saved, through faith—and this is not from your- selves, it is the gift of God." Eph. 2:8
9.		

We will conclude by contrasting two stories that directly addresses the lie: Grace Means I Have to Be Tolerant.

A Year's Worth of Grace

Ever have an annoying neighbor? Alexandru had one. A Christian in Romania, already facing all kinds of persecution for his faith, Alex came home tired from work each day to find his neighbor's trash in his yard. Every day for a year, Alex quietly picked up the trash and went about his life, trying to live at peace with everyone, as far as it depended on him (Rom. 12:18).

After a year had passed, Alexandru's neighbor approached him and said, "I don't understand. Every day I put my trash in your yard and you say nothing. How can you tolerate what I have done?"

"Because I serve a God that tells me not to fight back—to not return a wrong for a wrong."

"What kind of a God do you serve? I want to serve that same God."

"Come on over. I have a Bible. And I will show you the God that I serve."

Alex lived out his faith by extending grace, which resulted in an open door to share the gospel with his neighbor. What a powerful testimony without using words!

Yet, as we have highlighted in this chapter, we don't always know how that grace will be received, nor do we have a foolproof formula for when and how to show grace. In the following story, for example, grace meant drawing a line instead of turning the other cheek.

Permission to be Intolerant

My mom has always hated cigarette smoke. So when the across-the-street neighbor blew smoke in mom's face to accompany her refusal of the invitation to the neighborhood women's Bible study, mom was hesitant to invite her again. After a couple of years of open invitations and smoky rejections, mom stopped inviting. Of course, that's the year that Jackie came and knocked on mom's door to invite herself to the Bible study.

God worked a powerful transformation in the lives of all of those who lived in that house. Mom and dad studied the Bible with Jackie and her husband, Ted. There is no shortage of stories to share as our families became close friends, and even swapped houses to host Thanksgiving and Easter for many years.

Fast-forward about fifteen years… no longer neighbors, Jackie and my mom had stayed in touch as Christian sisters and friends. So when Jackie and her youngest son, Aaron, were facing some difficult times, they came to live with my parents in another state for a while.

Like we discussed in Chapter 10: "Lie: God is Punishing Me for My Past," Jackie had been freed from any guilt and punishment, but, unfortunately, her family still suffered some of the negative effects of past brokenness, and consequences of some prior decisions.

Aaron's now six foot, three inch, 250+ pound frame, coupled with a spike collar, gauge earrings and all-black clothing did little to soften his image or cover his insecurities. They only added to the intensity of his words when he verbally attacked my mom, disrespecting her, and making demands that were beyond my parents' ability.

"His words of disrespect caused my heart to pound in my chest, and really unnerved me."

After the first time, she extended him grace, seeking to see him beyond the hurt he was projecting as a burdened high school student. But after a second and third time, mom became more affected by Aaron's words and actions. He was spiraling and causing additional trouble and unnecessary issues for my parents.

They consulted both an elder and a deacon, and after much prayer decided that they had to draw the line. While they wanted to continue to show Aaron grace, they could not tolerate his behavior, especially the verbal abuse and disrespect of my mom.

Jackie continued to live with my parents for a few more days, but Aaron was no longer welcome in their home. During this time, they wrestled with the lie: Grace Means I Have to Be Tolerant, but came to recognize it as the lie that it was.

Thankfully, the prayers, love, grace, and truth that were shown to Aaron by my parents, by his mom, and by many others, brought about a transformation in Aaron's life. Years after the aforementioned incident, he contacted my parents and apologized for his words, his behavior, and his disrespect, thanking them for the grace and tough love they had shown him.

We thank God for the way this part of Aaron's story ended and continues to be written. We often don't get the privilege of knowing how it all turns out. We don't get "the rest of the story" of the woman caught in adultery (John 8). Some of the other stories in this final chapter of *Who Has the Last Word?* leave us hanging, with the anticipation of the unknown.

In the same way the watchman on the tower sounds the warning and leaves it to others to make their own decision, we have no control over another person's free will.

There is no perfect formula for how much grace to extend, or when to be intolerant and draw the line. Prayers for wisdom are vitally important as we all humbly seek God's will and His heart in our interaction with others.

Grace *and* truth. It's not an either/or. As long as we are the recipients of grace, we should also serve as the conduits of that grace to others. And when we have the knowledge of the truth, we are called to be intolerant of sin, yet not to the exclusion of love and grace when we live out and communicate that truth. "**Let your conversation be always full of grace, seasoned with salt, so that you may know how to answer everyone**" (Col. 4:6).

Common Threads

Since this is our final opportunity to share in the Common Threads, allow me to remind us of a bottom line truth we have highlighted in this chapter and throughout the entire book: **God's abundant grace washes over us as we wrestle with the lies. And His uncompromising truth frees us from the bondage of those lies. The God of grace and truth redeems us, blessing us with the abundant life He has promised, full of faith, hope, and love.** What are some final personal and practical steps you can take, supported by your Iron Rose Sisters, through the Common Threads?

An area in which you'd like to grow or bloom—abounding in faith, hope, and love through truth.

_____

_____

A thorn (lie) you'd like to remove and replace with truth.

_____

_____

An area in which you'd like to dig deeper or need someone to hold you accountable (help to recognize the lie or remember the truth).

_____

_____

A verse or truth to remember that speaks to a lie mentioned in this chapter.

_____

_____

Conclusion: Give Jesus the Closing Argument

You made it! Congratulations! I know this has not been an easy journey. When Satan knows that he is being called out as the liar he is, he is not happy. And he fights with an intensity and a vengeance that can leave us feeling weak and wounded. But, the good news? **Satan does not get the last word!**

We have a choice. And I pray that throughout the course of this interactive Bible study, you have gained some of the tools to give God the last word—tools with which you can recognize the lies, replace them with truth, and remember the truth through God's Word.

As our Mediator and Advocate, let's give Jesus the closing argument and allow the Word of God to be the last word that we rest in through love, cling to in hope, and remember daily to trust.

You are not in this spiritual battle alone. I have prayed over each of you and I hope that you have been able to go through this study in a small group context—with your Iron Rose Sisters, who have also lifted you up to the Father, like the exercise in chapter 6.

As a final reminder from each of the chapters, I have given you a final Lie/Truth Chart with the big lie from each chapter, and a key verse with which you can remember the truth. Please replace the lie with a truth, in your own words, and take advantage of the

Blank Lie/Truth Chart, found on page 293, that you can use as a "cheat sheet" when Satan attacks. Both this Master Lie/Truth Chart and a blank one are available for download on our website (www.IronRoseSister.com).

Thank you for joining on this journey together and for choosing to give God the last word in your life!

"May the grace of the Lord Jesus Christ, and the love of God, and the fellowship of the Holy Spirit be with you all," (2 Cor. 13:14) as you embrace the abundant life He offers. Amen.

RECOGNIZE the lie (in your own words)	REPLACE the lie with truth (in your own words)	REMEMBER the truth (biblical reference)
Chapter 6: I Am Alone		"I will never leave you nor forsake you." Josh. 1:5b
Chapter 7: Happiness is the Ultimate Goal		"But seek first his kingdom and his righteousness, and all these things will be given to you as well." Matt. 6:33
Chapter 8: I Have to Do it On My Own		"And I will ask the Father, and he will give you another advocate to help you and be with you forever— the Spirit of truth." John 14:16-17a

RECOGNIZE	REPLACE	REMEMBER
Chapter 9: Lies We Believe When We're Discouraged		"When my life was ebbing away, I remembered you, Lord, and my prayer rose to you, to your holy temple." **Jonah 2:7**
Chapter 10: God is Punishing Me for My Past		"as far as the east is from the west, so far has he removed our transgressions from us." **Ps. 103:12 (8-12)**
Chapter 11: I Am Not Enough		"But he said to me, 'My grace is sufficient for you, for my power is made perfect in weakness.'" **2 Cor. 12:9**
Chapter 12: Sexual Lies		"Run from sexual sin! No other sin so clearly affects the body as this one does. For sexual immorality is a sin against your own body." **1 Cor. 6:18 (NLT)**
Chapter 13: Grace Means I Have to be Tolerant		"The Word became flesh and made his dwelling among us... who came from the

		Father, full of grace and truth." **John 1:14**

Notes

Idaho Potato Cake[30]

1 cup butter, softened

2 cups sugar

2 eggs

1 cup cold mashed potatoes

1 tsp. vanilla

2 cups flour

1/4 cup baking cocoa

1 tsp. baking soda

1 cup milk (2%)

1 cup chopped nuts (optional)

In mixing bowl, cream margarine and sugar till fluffy, add eggs one at a time, beating well. Blend in potatoes and vanilla.

Combine flour, cocoa and baking soda. Add alternately with milk, blending well.

Stir in nuts (optional).

Pour into greased 9x13 pan. Bake 40-45 min at 350 degrees.

---

30 Capper, Arthur, pub., "Idaho Potato Cake," *Capper's Weekly*. Topeka, Kansas, 1913-1986. (unknown published date of original recipe)

Depression Resources from National Institute of Mental Health (NIMH)[31]

According to the NIMH, "people with depressive illnesses do not all experience the same symptoms. The severity, frequency, and duration of symptoms vary depending on the individual and his or her particular illness."

Signs and Symptoms include:

- ➢ Persistent sad, anxious, or "empty" feelings
- ➢ Feelings of hopelessness or pessimism
- ➢ Feelings of guilt, worthlessness, or helplessness
- ➢ Irritability, restlessness (more common in men)
- ➢ Loss of interest in activities or hobbies once pleasurable, including sex
- ➢ Fatigue and decreased energy
- ➢ Difficulty concentrating, remembering details, and making decisions

---

[31] https://www.nimh.nih.gov/health/topics/depression/index.shtml

> ➤ Insomnia, early-morning wakefulness, or excessive sleeping
> ➤ Overeating or appetite loss
> ➤ Thoughts of suicide, suicide attempts
> ➤ Aches or pains, headaches, cramps, or digestive problems that do not ease, even with treatment

When four or more of these symptoms are present for more than two weeks, it is recommended that one consult with a medical professional.

How can I help a loved one who is depressed?

If you know someone who is depressed, it affects you too. The most important thing you can do is help your friend or relative get a diagnosis and treatment. You may need to make an appointment and go with him or her to see the doctor. Encourage your loved one to stay in treatment, or to seek different treatment if no improvement occurs after 6 to 8 weeks.

To help your friend or relative:

> ➤ Offer emotional support, understanding, patience, and encouragement.
> ➤ Talk to him or her, and listen carefully.
> ➤ Never dismiss feelings, but point out realities and offer hope.
> ➤ Never ignore comments about suicide, and report them to your loved one's therapist or doctor.
> ➤ Invite your loved one out for walks, outings and other activities. Keep trying if he or she declines, but don't push him or her to take on too much too soon.
> ➤ Provide assistance in getting to the doctor's appointments.

> ➤ Remind your loved one that with time and treatment, the depression will lift.

How can I help myself if I am depressed?

If you have depression, you may feel exhausted, helpless, and hopeless. It may be extremely difficult to take any action to help yourself. But as you begin to recognize your depression and begin treatment, you will start to feel better.

To help yourself:

> ➤ Do not wait too long to get evaluated or treated. There is research showing the longer one waits, the greater the impairment can be down the road. Try to see a professional as soon as possible.
> ➤ Try to be active and exercise. Go to a movie, a ballgame, or another event or activity that you once enjoyed.
> ➤ Set realistic goals for yourself.
> ➤ Break up large tasks into small ones, set some priorities and do what you can as you can.
> ➤ Try to spend time with other people and confide in a trusted friend or relative. Try not to isolate yourself, and let others help you.
> ➤ Expect your mood to improve gradually, not immediately. Do not expect to suddenly "snap out of" your depression. Often during treatment for depression, sleep and appetite will begin to improve before your depressed mood lifts.
> ➤ Postpone important decisions, such as getting married or divorced or changing jobs, until you feel better. Discuss decisions with others who know you well and have a more objective view of your situation.

> ➤ Remember that positive thinking will replace negative thoughts as your depression responds to treatment.
> ➤ Continue to educate yourself about depression.

Additional Depression Resources and Biblical References

What To Say and What NOT To Say to Someone Battling Depression

NOT Say: Why don't you want to do anything?

DO Say: **Would you like to go for a walk with me?** (or some other simple invitation that you don't take personally if they decline)

NOT Say: This is dumb. You need to just get over it already.

DO Say: **I love you and I'm sorry you're going through this.**

NOT Say: Snap out of it!

DO Say: **You are not alone.**

NOT Say: It's just that your faith is weak.

DO Say: **It is hard to see you hurting and I wish I could fix it, but I will be here as a reminder of hope that God is bigger and that you will get better.**

NOT Say: You just need to pray/trust more.

DO Say: I am praying for you and I recognize that this is not just a spiritual battle, but also a physical/mental/emotional battle.

Depression and Discouragement in the Bible

Is depression addressed in the Bible? Yes! In addition to those mentioned in chapter 9: Lies We Believe When We're Discouraged, here are a few more examples of those who faced a time of depression or intense discouragement. For added reflection on the following biblical examples, I encourage you to ask questions like:

➤ What caused their depression/discouragement?
➤ How did they come out of it? And did they do it alone?
➤ This is not an exhaustive list. Who else can you think of?

Biblical Examples of Depression and Discouragement

➤ Elijah ~ 1 Kings 19
➤ Joshua ~ Joshua 1:9
  o Caused by fear
➤ Paul ~ 2 Corinthians 12:7-10
  o Thorn in the flesh: a physical annoyance or a disability
➤ David ~ 2 Samuel 12 & Psalm 51
  o Caused by his guilt (adultery) and the disease of his son
➤ The disciples ~ Luke 24:36-49; John 20:19-20
  o Until Jesus arrived (Acts)
➤ Hannah ~ 1 Samuel 1
  o Longing for a child
➤ Ruth vs. Naomi ~ Ruth 1

- o Bitterness of soul
- o Naomi even wanted her name changed to Mara (bitter)
➤ Peter vs. Judas ~ Matthew 26-28
- o Matthew 26:14-16, 47-50, 69-75; 27:3-10, Acts

Conquering and Overcoming Discouragement

➤ More than conquerors ~ Romans 8:37-39
➤ The Holy Spirit dwells in you ~ Acts 2:38
- o Depression is not the indwelling of a demon
➤ In trials ~ Job (Job 1:20-22)
➤ Recognize the will of God
- o Jesus in Gethsemane (Matt. 26:36-46)
➤ Recognize God's strength
- o Ex. David and Goliath (1 Sam. 17)
➤ God is light in the darkness ~ Psalm 112:4
➤ He lifts us up ~ Ephesians 5:13-14
➤ Walk by faith, not by sight ~ 2 Corinthians 5:7
➤ See the spiritual, not the physical ~ 2 Corinthians 4:16-18
➤ Keep your eyes fixed on Jesus ~ Hebrews 12:2

What encourages you, strengthens you or gives you joy?

➤ Sing ~ Ephesians 5:19
➤ Give thanks ~ Ephesians 5:20
➤ Pray ~ Ephesians 6:18; James 5:13
➤ Put on the full armor of God ~ Ephesians 6:10-17
➤ Remember God's promises ~ Isaiah 41:10
➤ Work for the Lord ~ Ezra 10:4
➤ Love – given and received ~ 1 John 4:7-12
➤ Encourage others ~ Hebrews 10:23-26

- ➤ Rejoice ~ Philippians 4:4, James 1:3
- ➤ Preach ~ Philippians 1:14, 2 Timothy 4:17
- ➤ Listen to God ~ Daniel 10:15-19
- ➤ Listen to Jesus, "take heart" with healings, fear, and forgiveness ~ Matthew 9:2, 22; 14:27 and others
- ➤ See God in you ~ 1 John 4:4
- ➤ Comfort ~ 2 Corinthians 1:3-7
- ➤ Strength of God ~ Psalm 31:1-5

Other Key Uplifting Verses

- ➤ 1 Chronicles 28:20
- ➤ Lamentations 3:19-24, 33, 55-57
- ➤ Ephesians 3:14-21
- ➤ 2 Corinthians 4:7-12, 16-18
- ➤ Isaiah 61:1-4
- ➤ John 3:14-15
- ➤ Romans 8:18, 15:13
- ➤ Nehemiah 8:10 ~ the joy of the Lord

Libby's Story

If a spider's web were one straight line, very few insects would fall prey and be devoured by the spider. While God draws clear lines about sin and abundant life through His word, **Satan weaves a web of lies, making it easier for us to fall into the "grey" areas.** Sometimes that web spans large amounts of time, growing ever wider with each new lie, ever increasing the chances that God's children will unexpectedly find themselves struggling in the sticky trap, as Satan creeps up to devour us. **Satan pursued me for many years, weaving a special web of lies for me that tore down my self worth.**

Up until I graduated college, my life was headed in the "right" direction. I worked hard at the university, happily walked across the arena floor to accept my diploma, and shortly thereafter boarded a plane to Honduras as I had the previous summers of my college career. I was the mission-minded, servant-hearted, church-going gal. That is not to say that I was without sin. On the contrary, I struggled with sin; but I never felt that Satan had a life-altering hold on my heart. Looking back, **I see that Satan slowly reeled me in—inch by inch, relationship by relationship, he tugged on me. Before I knew it, I didn't even recognize myself.**

Just before graduating and moving to Honduras (until the political instability sent me home), I met a man who took an interest in me. I was excited because that didn't happen often. In high school, I didn't date. No one pursued me—which really got me **feeling like I was undesirable. Sometimes I let that thought consume me, and Satan started planting seeds of doubt about my value and worth.** I didn't realize how my thoughts about myself were changing at first, until I found myself in a relationship. **Lie #1: My worth and value comes from men.**

In college, I had an undefined, long-distance relationship with a Christian guy. Throughout that very ambiguous time, I felt my heart breaking in ways that later caused me to not protect my heart. The man I dated never wanted to define our relationship. In public, we looked like the best of friends—we were happy and playful. I really adored him, and he was clearly affectionate toward me. Many people commented that we should be a couple, and encouraged it. In private, we enjoyed each other's company, and crossed several physical boundaries we shouldn't have, although we never had sex. I often asked him to give our relationship a definition that the world would understand: a couple, boyfriend and girlfriend. But he always had an excuse for waiting to define it, and I blindly accepted each one, clinging to the relationship when I should have walked away. **I was scared of letting go for fear there wasn't something better for me.** During the last chunk of time we were separated, he found a new girlfriend and proudly displayed their relationship. I was devastated. I had been his secret girlfriend—he wasn't proud enough of me to tell everyone about our relationship. Was he ashamed of me in some way? Or was he just taking advantage of me? Now Satan seized his opportunity to really rob me of my self-confidence. **Lie #2: No man will take pride in having me by his side.**

That relationship was a catalyst for how I engaged in future relationships. Perhaps the saddest result of that relationship was that it soured me on dating Christian men. It did not completely deter me, but I began to think, if someone so active in the faith could treat me so poorly, then what is the difference between dating a Christian man, and dating a man who is not Christian? So Satan planted another lie in my mind. **Lie #3: It is okay to be in a relationship with someone who does not share my faith and convictions.**

Fast forward again, back to the man who took an interest in me at the end of my college career. He had many qualities I desired. He was educated, working on his master's degree. He came from a good family with similar values as mine. He was a deep-thinker, and I found him attractive, among other things. He was raised in a Catholic family, though he did not practice Catholicism on a regular basis. **From what I could tell, he was not pursuing a relationship with God. This is when I should have walked away. But, wait! TA-DA! Here I was, placed in his path to be an example of God's love! Yes! This was true—I could have been a great Christian friend for him. But what did I do? I suppressed my eagerness to see him pursue a relationship with God in order to pursue a romantic relationship with him. Even more shameful, I justified my actions instead of changing them.** He believed in God. He knew Jesus to be the Son of God and our Savior. So, I wasn't starting from zero. The foundation was there for developing the spiritual side of our relationship. Honestly, though, I wasn't trying to develop that side at all. In fact, I feared that bringing up matters of salvation, and digging even a little below the surface, would drive him away. I craved the male attention, and later on in our relationship, gave into the physical temptation. I abandoned my convictions and starting having sex with him.

Once that physical line was crossed, I clung to the relationship. I felt obligated to stay, even when it became apparent that this was not a person with whom to build my future. **I didn't want to admit that sex was a big mistake. I wanted it to mean something.** I wanted it to mean we were in love. How naive of me. I'm almost embarrassed to admit: that thought crossed my mind as a college-educated adult. Nonetheless, the relationship ended when my boyfriend graduated and moved home. Nothing I had done had convinced him to stay. **Lie #4: Sex will save your relationship.**

Some time later, I found myself living in a new city. I thought of this transition as a clean slate. I didn't have intentions of going wild and crazy, but I was open to new experiences, new relationships, and new friends. I was excited to explore a new place and meet a lot of different people, which my job allowed me to do. I quickly sought out a church home, and began attending a girls' Bible study. I settled in. Shortly after moving, I met someone and we quickly began spending a lot of time together. Our relationship moved fast, and I did little to try and slow it down. **All those lies Satan wove for me throughout my other relationships finally compounded. Without even knowing it, I believed them.** I was done protecting my heart because I didn't see the point. It wasn't long before I was right smack in the same place I was with my previous boyfriend, but the consequences this time were much greater.

Some consequences of sin go unnoticed by the people around you. That was true for me, until I got pregnant. Before I became pregnant, I attended church regularly, as well as the girls' Bible study. **I was often confronted with the truth through the topics we discussed and scriptures we read, especially in the more intimate setting of a girls' small group, but I chose not to let it change my actions.** Perhaps people around me noticed something was different, but they also didn't know me very well. Since I was new to the area, they were just getting to know me. They knew things about me—what I did for a living, where I had traveled— bits of information here and there.

I didn't make myself vulnerable to them by sharing the struggle I was experiencing with my boyfriend. Perhaps because, in the beginning, I chose not to see it as a struggle. I had been the "good girl" for many years. That's not to say that I turned "bad," but I gave up resisting Satan. I gave in, once again, and barreled into a sexual relationship shortly after I began dating my boyfriend. **I still spent time in prayer, and personal study, but I purposefully ignored the truth when it came to sex.** I knew that people in the church would encourage me to give up the sexual nature of our relationship, and perhaps even to ditch the whole relationship. I knew that they would challenge me to think about the consequences (not just the physical ones), and to consider the spiritual side of a relationship with this man. Truthfully, the spiritual side didn't exist. He believed in God, but again, was not someone who lived out his faith (a tragic theme in my relation- ships).

Not too long into the relationship, the guilt overpowered the pleasure. After about four months together, I decided to end the sexual part of our relationship. I wanted to be right with God. I wanted peace. So, I told him, no more. It felt good to finally say it, and mean it. I worried I would not be able to stop. I had talked to him on other occasions about ending our physical relationship, just as I had done with my previous boyfriend. But sex is a slippery slope, and in both relationships, we always seemed to roll down it again. This time, I told myself I could not give in. I had taken the first step, and I felt resolved to see it through. Those good feelings were short-lived. A week or two later, I realized I was pregnant. My effort to change my behavior—to right the wrong and avoid the consequences—was too late. And so Satan dug in deep and sent me spiraling into the darkest depression of my life.

Since I lived far from my family. I had to tell my parents I was pregnant over the phone. They had not even met my boyfriend. Everyone was shocked: my siblings, my parents, and my friends. Everyone. They knew me as the daughter, sister, and friend who had plans to work serving God in Central America. I was overwhelmed by the thought of facing people I had served alongside in the mission field, people I grew up with in the youth group, their parents, former teachers and classmates. I had marred my own reputation. Part of me was relieved to be so far from home, because I couldn't randomly bump into people I knew out in public. I was so ashamed.

Then, I started thinking about all the ways my life was about to change—all the big ideas and plans I had for my future that seemed unattainable, given my new circumstances. I began grieving the life I thought I would have. Worry set in as I began assessing the cost of raising a child. I was not financially prepared to bring a child into the world. Financial worries aside; **I was even more consumed by the idea that I didn't have enough love for my child.** I worried that I was so emotionally depleted that I would not be able to muster the love my child needed to be emotionally healthy. Not to mention that his father and I were struggling in our relationship, to say the least. Guilt and sadness consumed me. There was no one to blame but me. I had done it to myself.

At the same time, I was experiencing a spiritual crisis. As if the whole situation didn't scream spiritual crisis, I had a very specific, recurring thought for many months. I was not spared the consequence of my actions, and **I began to doubt that God had grace and mercy for me. I felt neglected by God, even though I had alienated myself from Him.**

My grief was not only defined by sadness, but by anger. Anger so foreign to me, I scared myself. I wish I could say that when my son was born, my sadness and anger was drowned out by joy and love. It was a joyful time, yes, because children are a blessing. But I was still struggling to accept my new life.

About a month after my son was born, I started keeping a journal. It helped me be more honest with myself and with God about how I was feeling at the time. This is part of my first entry:

Today I feel defeated. **The Bible says the wages of sin is death.** *I always imagined a physical death, not this slow, emotional demise that eats away at the person I was when I lived in the Light. I miss Honduras. I miss the happy, confident person I was when my life was defined by Christ and not by men who steal pieces of me as I try to make myself pleasing to them. How did I get here? How did I become this person consumed by anger, void of confidence and pursued by grief?* **Why didn't I believe and bask in God's love instead of trying to find it and make it in all the wrong beds?** *But who wouldn't cling to the hints and allusions of interest from a man when you feel, or fear rather, that 'if I don't try to make it work with him, no one else will want me.' I regret not standing with confidence. I regret accepting less than what I deserved. I* *regret trying to force love when I knew I had it all along—in Christ, not in man.*

My journal quickly evolved into a prayer journal, and I found peace in working out my thoughts and petitions in writing. Taking the time to write kept me focused, and my prayers became more Scripture-based. As I spent more time with God, His Word began to live in me again, and more so than it had in the past. He reminded me, in those conversations, of His love and grace, that I thought I had lost. I found comfort in several scriptures, but there were a handful that I revisited often:

"The Lord will fight for you; you need only to be still" (Ex. 14:14).

Lie #5: I often felt that because I got myself into this mess, I had to get myself out. I made God small and myself busy with worry. I fixated on all the things I could have done to change my circumstances. When I finally put it in God's hands, on a consistent basis, I was able to experience peace. **A recurring theme in my prayers was: YOU ARE BIGGER!** In capital letters, just like that. **I had to remind myself of that truth often.** I am a doer. I don't like to be idle, but God was almost forcing me to be still so I could let him fight.

"The Lord your God is in your midst, a mighty one who will save; he will rejoice over you with gladness; he will quiet you by his love; he will exult over you with loud singing" (Zeph. 3:17, ESV).

"Humble yourselves, therefore, under God's mighty hand, that he may lift you up in due time. Cast all your anxiety on him because he cares for you" (1 Peter 5:6-7, TNIV).

"Let the morning bring me word of your unfailing love, for I have put my trust in you. Show me the way I should go, for to you I entrust my life. Rescue me from my enemies, Lord, for I hide myself in you. Teach me to do your will, for you are my God; may your good Spirit lead me on level ground" (Ps. 143:8-10).

Not only did I seek comfort in the Word of God, but also in fellowship with my church family. When I finally told the girls in my Bible study that I was pregnant, I felt so relieved. They were prayer warriors for me, and loved me through it. I only regret that I didn't tell them earlier on in the pregnancy. I sought counsel from a trusted minister and friend who asked me the tough questions, not to condemn me, but to challenge me and motivate me toward healing. **As a woman, the gift of Christian sisters is irreplaceable. I am so thankful for the fellowship and trust I found in them.**

While I remain grateful for my church family in the city where I was living, in the months after my son was born, I decided to move home. It became apparent to me that I could not make the forward progress I needed staying where I was. I needed the support of my physical family. I needed some distance from the situation that kept dragging me down. Packing up and leaving my son's father behind was the hardest decision I ever made. The separation caused a different kind of pain, but I had peace in knowing that my decision was motivated by God and the desire to make the best life for my son. I knew that God would bless that decision, and He already has in many ways. The physical distance allowed for mental clarity. Just having a clear mind settled some of the worry and fear I was experiencing.

I began to feel peace as I acknowledged God's power. He is bigger than my sin, bigger than my circumstances. I dubbed Him the 'author of change' in my life. Each time that I acknowledge His power, I feel my faith stretching, growing. He continues to bring about positive changes in my life, none of which I can take credit for. **It is by His power and grace that I am no longer trapped in Satan's web of lies.** Not only that, but He has empowered me to forgive myself, and those men who did not show me the respect I deserved. I am no longer burdened by bitterness and anger toward them. I take responsibility for my actions, and recognize the ways by which Satan deceived me. He still tries to make me feel worthless. One of the biggest lies he told me was that my value and my worth came from men. I know that isn't true, but on the days when Satan is bearing down hard, I read Psalm 139. I am fearfully and wonderfully made! My Creator knows me completely, and loves me anyway! This chapter reminds me to love myself because I am a wonderful creation of God. It motivates me to see other people in the same way, and to accept them where they are on their journey. Many people accepted me at the lowest point in my life, so I will do the same for others. I can bask in the truth of God's perfect, unconditional love, and spread it around more abundantly. **I can stand with confidence again knowing my worth is as a child of God, not a girlfriend of man.**

I am still navigating the unknown, and working toward a more positive future. After moving home, I made the decision to pursue a more family-friendly career. God paved the path for this new pursuit, and I am thankful to be back on track, looking forward to the future instead of weighed down by the past. I am rebuilding and growing, seeking God's wisdom and peace in the tough decisions. There are days I battle fiercely to not let myself slip back into that dark place. I take comfort in knowing I am not alone. God's greatest reminder of that is my son. He is a vessel of God's unconditional love, hope, and joy! When he covers my face in kisses, squeezes my neck in hugs, and kisses his own hand incessantly, blowing kisses when I leave for work, I am reminded of my greatest purpose on this earth now—to raise my son to love God, love himself, and love people. Of course, I also plan to teach him how to treat a lady with the respect she deserves.

About the Author

Michelle J. Goff has been writing small group Bible study materials in English and in Spanish throughout her ministry career. God has led Michelle to share these resources with more women across the world through Iron Rose Sister Ministries, a registered non-profit. She also continues to take advantage of opportunities for speaking engagements, seminars, women's retreats, and other women's ministry events across the Americas, in both English and in Spanish. If you would like to book a seminar in your area, please contact Michelle at ironrosesister@gmail.com, or for more information, visit www.IronRoseSister.com.

Personal Life

Michelle grew up in Baton Rouge, Louisiana, with her parents and three younger sisters. Her love and desire for helping women in their journey began early with her sisters, even when they thought she was being bossy. They've all grown a lot from those early years, but the sisterly bonds remain. Michelle has been blessed by the support of her family through all of her endeavors over the years.

Michelle enjoys time with family, cheering on the Atlanta Braves and the Louisiana State University Tigers, having coffee with friends, movies, travel, and speaking Spanish. And guess what her favorite flower is? Yep. The red rose.

She currently resides in Searcy, Arkansas, near her parents.

Ministry and Educational Experience

Michelle first felt called into ministry during her senior year at Harding University while obtaining a Bachelor of Arts degree in Communication Disorders and Spanish. She planned to join a team to plant a church in north Bogotá, Colombia, so she moved to Atlanta after graduating in May 1999 to facilitate that church-plant. Even though the plan for a Bogotá team fell through, Michelle continued her dream to be a part of a church plant there, which happened in March 2000.

She worked in the missions ministry at the North Atlanta Church of Christ for eighteen months before moving to Denver to work with English- and Spanish-speaking church plants there (Highlands Ranch Church of Christ and three Spanish-speaking congregations). During her two-and-a-half years there, Michelle continued her involvement in Bogotá and throughout various regions of Venezuela, visiting new church plants, teaching classes, conducting women's retreats, and speaking at and volunteering with youth camps.

In March 2003, Michelle moved to Caracas, Venezuela, to assist with a church planting on the eastern side of the city. Her time in Caracas was focused on the East Caracas congregation, but she was also able to participate in other women's activities across the country. In the four years Michelle spent in Caracas, the congregation grew from the twelve people meeting in her apartment to almost 100 meeting in a hotel conference room. The East Caracas congregation recently celebrated its twelfth anniversary and is still going strong in spite of the difficult economic and political situation in the country. A visit to Bogotá every three months to renew her Venezuelan visa also facilitated continued assistance with the congregation there.

In March 2007, Michelle transitioned back into ministry in the United States as the women's campus minister for the South Baton Rouge Church of Christ at the Christian Student Center (CSC) near the LSU campus. While walking with the college students on their spiritual journey and serving in other women's ministry roles, Michelle also pursued her "nerdy passion" of Spanish. She graduated from LSU in December 2011 with a Masters in Hispanic Studies, Linguistics Concentration. Her thesis explored the influence of social and religious factors in the interpretation of Scripture.

Michelle is now following God's calling to use her bilingual ministry experience with women of all ages and cultural backgrounds to bless them with opportunities for growth and deep spiritual connection with other Christian sisters through Iron Rose Sister Ministries.

About Iron Rose Sister
Ministries

Vision:

To equip women to connect to God and one another more deeply.

Overall Mission:

A ministry that facilitates Christian sister relationships that will be like iron sharpening iron, encouraging and inspiring each other to be as beautiful as a rose in spite of a few thorns. Its goal is to provide women's Bible studies that are simple enough for anyone to lead and yet, deep enough for everyone to grow. These resources are available in English and Spanish (Iron Rose Sister Ministries - IRSM/Ministerio Hermana Rosa de Hierro - MHRH).

FACETS of Iron Rose Sister Ministries' vision:

F – Faithfulness – to God above all else. First and foremost: *"Seek first His kingdom and His righteousness and all these things will be added to you as well"* (Matt. 6:33).

A – Authenticity – We're not hypocrites, just human. *"But he said to me, "My grace is sufficient for you, for my power is made perfect in weakness." Therefore I will boast all the more gladly about my weaknesses, so that Christ's power may rest on me. That is why, for Christ's sake, I delight in weaknesses, in insults, in hardships, in persecutions, in difficulties. For when I am weak, then I am strong"* (2 Cor. 12:9-10).

C – Community – We were not created to have an isolated relationship with God. He has designed the church as a body with many parts (1 Cor. 12). The magnitude of "one another" passages in the New Testament affirms this design. As women, we have unique relational needs at various stages in life—whether we are going through a time in which we need, like Moses, our arms raised in support by others (Ex. 17:12) or are able to rejoice with those who rejoice and mourn with those who mourn (Rom. 12:15). The Iron Rose Sister Ministries studies are designed to be shared in community.

E – Encouragement through Prayer and Accountability – *"As iron sharpens iron, so one person sharpens another"* (Prov. 27:17). God has not left us alone in this journey. *"Confess your sins to each other and pray for each other so that you may be healed. The prayer of a righteous man is powerful and effective"* (James 5:16). It is our prayer that every woman that joins in this mission participates as an Iron Rose Sister with other women, partnering in prayer and loving accountability.

T – Testimony – We all have a "God story." By recognizing his living and active hand in our lives, we are blessed to share that message of hope with others (John 4:39-42). Thankfully, that story is not over! God continues to work in the transformation of lives, and we long to hear your story.

S – Study – *"The Word of God is alive and active. Sharper than any double-edged sword, it penetrates even to dividing soul and spirit, joints and marrow; it judges the thoughts and attitudes of the heart"* (Heb. 4:12).

In order to fully realize the blessing, benefit, and design of the Iron Rose Sister Ministries vision, we must go to the Creator. Through a greater knowledge of the Word, we can blossom as roses and remove a few thorns—discerning the leading of the Spirit, recognizing the voice of the Father, and following the example of the Son. This is more effectively accomplished in community (small group Bible studies), but not to the exclusion of time alone with God (personal Bible study).

For more information, please:

Visit www.IronRoseSister.com.

Sign up for the IRSM daily blog and monthly newsletter.

IRSM is a registered 501(c)(3) public nonprofit with a board of directors and advisory eldership.

Bibliography

Bonhoeffer, Dietrich. *The Cost of Discipleship*. New York: Simon and Schuster, 1959.

Capper, Arthur, pub., "Idaho Potato Cake," *Capper's Weekly*. Topeka, Kansas, 1913-1986. (unknown published date of original recipe)

Cowell, Maria. "Porn: Women Use It Too," *Today's Christian Woman* online, February 2015, http://www.todayschristian woman.com/articles/2015/february-week-3/porn-women-use-it-too.html

Dalbey, Gordon. *Healing the Masculine Soul*. Nashville: Thomas Nelson, 2003.

Green, Michael P., ed. *1500 Illustrations for Biblical Preaching*. Grand Rapids: Baker Books, 2005.

Keller, Timothy. *Counterfeit Gods*. London: Penguin, 2009.

Lewis, C. S. *Mere Christianity*. New York: Harper Collins, 2001.

National Institute of Mental Health, https://www.nimh.nih.gov/health/topics/depression/index.shtml

Prochnow, Hebert V. and Hebert V. Prochnow, Jr. *5100 Quotations for Speakers and Writers*. Grand Rapids: Baker Books, 1992.

Rowell, Edward K. and *Leadership*, editors. *1001 Quotes, Illustrations, and Humorous Stories*. Grand Rapids: Baker Books, 2008.

Blank Lie/Truth Chart

RECOGNIZE the lie (in your own words)	REPLACE the lie with truth (in your own words)	REMEMBER the truth (biblical reference)

RECOGNIZE the lie (in your own words)	REPLACE the lie with truth (in your own words)	REMEMBER the truth (biblical reference)

Made in the USA
Coppell, TX
28 September 2022

83764276R00182